DATE			

FROM THE GHETTO TO THE GAMES
JEWISH ATHLETES IN HUNGARY

Andrew Handler

EAST EUROPEAN MONOGRAPHS, BOULDER
DISTRIBUTED BY COLUMBIA UNIVERSITY PRESS, NEW YORK
1985

EAST EUROPEAN MONOGRAPHS, NO. CXCII

CONTENTS

INTRODUCTION

Four main reasons prompted me to undertake the writing of this book. First, I wanted to set the record straight. Chaim Bermant wrote a long overdue chapter, "Not Playing the Game," on Jewish participation in sports in his highly entertaining book, *The Jews*. It aroused my curiosity by way of bruising my pride. He observed: "Apart from horse-racing (which could be more aptly described as an industry), the Jewish achievement in sport has been less than monumental and, compared to its achievements elsewhere, derisory." I do not know how widespread this view is, but I would dearly love to see the facial expression of any of the Jewish Olympic, world, European, or national champions upon reading these words. As for comparison, what is its true measure? Are the achievements of brain comparable to the achievements of brawn? Is a Jewish athlete's winning of an Olympic medal or finishing first at a world-class competition less of an achievement than an intellectual Jew's contribution to the arts or the sciences? Can any measure of comparison be valid? Indeed, should comparisons be made at all? I am inclined to give a negative response to the last question, which makes it unnecessary to address the preceding ones. The achievements of Jewish athletes are well respected, especially in the more receptive atmosphere of appreciation of physical values which the birth of Israel, the establishment of its areas of economic production, and the succession of four wars in the Middle East created.

My second motive in writing this book was that of nostalgia. Notwithstanding its numerous areas of inaccuracy and lacunae, the *Encyclopedia of Jews in Sports* of Bernard Postal, Jesse Silver, and Roy Silver is still the best reference work on the subject and, I believe, obviates the necessity

v

for a more comprehensive tome. Thus without much hesitation I gave in to a most pleasurable compulsion born of personal experience. Attempting to write about any field of athletic endeavor without the benefit of some practical experience is no less potentially self-defeating than attempting to learn how to play the sport from a book of dos and don'ts. The knowledge of the mechanics of any sport is no substitute for actual achievement. Moreover the sweat and blood of training and the feelings that travel the whole spectrum of emotions between exhilaration and desperation during competition leave an indelible impression that one treasures for a lifetime. In my case the quality of athletic achievement was of no decisive importance. As a member of the junior soccer team of *MATEOSZ* (the Hungarian Teamsters Union), and later a member of the under twenty-one tennis team of the Újpesti Dózsa, one of Hungary's most popular sport clubs, I learned enough of both sports to find them immensely enjoyable. To this day I remember my modest achievements, which were rewarded by a few small trophies and brief citations, with fondness.

In retrospect, my most satisfying accomplishment was the successful though short-lived blending of athletic fervor and religious conviction. It was difficult for me, then a student of the Boys' High School of the Budapest Jewish community, to play in an environment not known for philo-Semitic tendencies—even though at one stage of my soccer career six of my teammates were members of the *Maccabi ha-Za'ir* Zionist youth organization. The competitive spirit is not best retained amid choruses of anti-Semitic profanities and showers of well-aimed spit. My experiences as a student of Hungary's prestigious National Rabbinical Seminary playing competitive tennis in the Újpesti Dózsa, then the team of the National Police, were only slightly more uplifting. Still, as a direct result of my exposure to competitive tennis and soccer the sighting of any round object that may be kicked or hit with another object elicits an instantenious kinetic reaction in me. As an additional consequence I possess an unabating respect—coupled with only a mild case of envy—for the outstanding practitioners of all sports. This mixture of personal experience and persistent admiration inevitably increased my resolve to tell the story of the Hungarian-Jewish athletes as fully as the difficulties inherent in such an undertaking allowed.

My third reason for writing this book reinforces the second. Even a cursory glance at the entry "Olympic Games" in the *Encyclopedia Judaica,* which contains a list of all Jewish athletes who won Olympic medals between 1896 and 1968, reveals an unusually frequent recurrence of Hungary as the national origin of the athletes cited. The numbers attest to a string of remarkable achievements. Jewish athletes from Hungary won nearly one-third of all Olympic medals (236) awarded to Jewish competitors, nearly half of all gold medals, and only one less (76) than all the medals won by Jewish athletes from both the United States and the Soviet Union. Additional Hungarian-Jewish competitors not identified by the compilers of the Olympic statistics will make these percentage figures look even more impressive.

The documentation of Olympic achievements, however, reveals only the tip of the iceberg. Hungarian-Jewish athletes have amassed a truly extraordinary number of titles, medals, and records in competition of other kinds as well, in world, European, and national championships.

The description of Jewish achievement in sport rarely amounts to more than a brief contribution to a volume of essays or a chapter in a work on the general history of Jews or a national Jewish community. The achievements of Hungarian-Jewish athletes constitute an unparalleled chapter in the annals of Jewish history. They have been so extraordinarily varied and successful that to recount them within the confines of an essay or a chapter would not only reduce them to a mere statistical accounting—a gross injustice under the circumstances—but would also gloss over one of the most colorful and telling aspects of Hungarian-Jewish history.

Finally, the convergence of a number of circumstances prompted me to look forward to the labors of researching and writing the book with optimism. The realization that no comparable work on the contributions of a national Jewish community to sport was extant provided a constant stream of intellectual and emotional stimuli. The gathering of data, however, was a bag of mixed blessings—at times satisfying and successful, at times frustrating and unyielding. When I turned to the literature on the topic of Hungarian sport, I encountered a number of problems that will be discussed in the Bibliographical Notes. A collateral branch of the traditional data collecting process, the acquisition of information through interviews, turned out to be similarly intriguing in the diversity of its results. The correspondence I was able to sustain with a number of former Hungarian-Jewish athletic luminaries revealed a variety of responses. Predictably, their remarks were not unanimously supportive of my project.

Some were enthusiastic and cooperative, but others preferred not to bring their Jewishness to public attention. Their athletic achievement, they felt, should be recognized solely within the Hungarian context. Still others ignored my initiative altogether, and one flatly denied Jewish origin despite documentary evidence and common knowledge to the contrary.

The most exasperating dilemma, one from which I could not entirely extricate myself, was the direct result of the shortcomings of the written sources and the misinformation which my contributors had inadvertently provided. The identification game is in many respects the most decisive criterion of success in the preparation of a book of this kind. Its mastery, however, often remains an elusive goal. Many Jews in Hungary retained their Germanic family names. So did many non-Jewish Hungarians of German origin. Conversely, since the beginning of the quick-paced Magyarization in the latter part of the nineteenth century many Jews and non-Jews adopted Magyar family names. The accuracy of identification in encyclopedias and other written sources, the memories of well-informed members of the Jewish community—where the answers to who is a Jew and who is not have been placed for safekeeping—and the clues that the combination of certain family and given names provide sometimes proved less than reliable.

The inherent difficulties of the identification procedure persisted and remained unresolved in the face of all reasonable professional research techniques. I was, therefore, compelled in a few instances to include or exclude on grounds that to some readers, I expect, will appear arbitrary or even unjustified. There of course exists a narrow margin of error, for no compiler of lists ever succeeds in eliminating it. Moreover, I chose not to proceed with the selection process in strict conformity to the prevailing definitions of a Jew as a person who declares himself or herself a Jew, or was born of a Jewish mother, or converted to Judaism. Such criteria will simply not suffice with respect to societies in which the public declaration of one's Jewishness is a serious impediment to advancement, success, and acceptance. I have been told—and I also am a witness to the veracity of the statement—that many Jewish athletes kept quiet about, concealed, and even denied their religious background for that reason. Others pretended that they had converted to Christianity or were Christian-born. (In socialist countries it is, at least in theory if not always in practice, a moot point altogether.) There undoubtedly were compelling personal reasons for resorting to such subterfuge. In the absence of freedom and protection, one's instincts of self-preservation must surely override considerations of morality and even the possible loss of self-respect. Thus my principal objective was to exclude those athletes who were neither born of Jewish parents nor converted to Judaism (many such individuals have mistakenly been included in some routinely unchallenged lists) rather than impose the yoke of Jewishness on persons who cannot or do not wish to accept it. Therefore, as the objective of this book is the documentation of athletic achievement as a barometer of the degree of assimilation, rather than the mere statistical compilation and quantitative analysis of data, I chose to omit those individuals whose religious identity was a matter of dispute and could not be verified with reasonable certainty.

Through the researching and writing of this book I was all too conscious of the mounting debt I owe a small group of individuals who were my source of support and information. Professor Alexander Scheiber, Director of the National Rabbinical Seminary, Budapest, Hungary; Éva Székely, a former Olympic, European, and national champion swimmer and coach; István Sárkány, a former national champion gymnast and coach of the Hungarian national gymnastics team, Sándor Loewy, a former goalkeeper of the Hungarian *VAC* and the Austrian Hakoah soccer teams; László Bellák, a former world and national champion table tennis player; Emery Kálmán of Los Angeles; and Professor George Eisen of the California State Polytechnic University. I am greatly indebted to my mother for identifying the religious origin of many a Hungarian athlete and for typing the manuscript; and to my wife for her encouragement and for listening with patience and fortitude to the sport stories of my youth. To Hilde L. Robinson I wish to acknowledge my gratitude for her meticulous work in editing the manuscript.

NOTE ON PRONUNCIATION

Readers unfamiliar with the Hungarian language might find the following guide useful in attempting to pronounce Hungarian names and terms.

1. Stress is placed invariably on the first syllable.
2. The letter r is the so-called trilled r. It is pronounced by vibrating the tongue while touching it to the front of the roof of the mouth.
3. Consonants:

Letter	Sound	Example
c and cz	tz	kibitz
cs	ch	pinch
g	g	golf (even before e and i)
gy	di	Nadia
j and ly	y	yoke
s	sh	shop
sz	s	skin
ty	tth	Matthew
sz	zh	bijou

4. Vowels:

Letter	Sound	Example
a	aw	raw
á	i	night
i	i	pick
í	ee	peek

Vowels (continued)

Letter	Sound	Example
o	o	score
ó	oa	moat
ö and eö	u	curt
ő	eu	French feu
u	oo	wood
ú	oo	moose
ü	u	French tu
ű	ue	French rue

CHAPTER I

THE "NEW JEWS"

Toward the end of the ninth century, wandering Magyar tribes reached the former central-European, Roman province of Pannonia. It has been a prolonged and circuitous sojourn, beginning in western Siberia. The Magyars, conquering Pannonia and settling on the land, soon shaped a heroic age as the vision of a permanent national state began to emerge. Late nineteenth-century Hungarian historians concluded that the arrival of the Magyars in their future homeland took place between 888 and 900. To commemorate the event, the government of Count István Tisza designated 1896 as the millennial year and proceeded to organize a celebration.

It was an appropriate and timely decision. By the turn of the century, Hungary had capped the initial phase of its long-overdue entry into the industrial age. The ambitious architects of the country's fast-paced development paused to remember the heroic founding fathers: Árpád, the tribal chief, his seven vezirs, and the kings of the House of Árpád, and pay solemn tribute to a nation chastised by Mongol, Turkish, and Austrian masters. The mood, however, was robustly and confidently optimistic. Hungary had greatly benefited from the Austrians' embarrassing, albeit predictable, defeat at the hands of the Prussians in 1866. Emperor Francis Joseph reluctantly consented to the administrative overhaul of his realm that culminated in the compromise (*Ausgleich*) of the dual monarchy of Austria-Hungary. Even though the ministries of foreign affairs, defense, and finance were under Austrian control, Hungarians would take pride in

1

those aspects of political life, such as the constitution, the bicameral parliament, and domestic affairs, over which they retained jurisdiction. There was an atmosphere of near-independence, even if it was largely illusory.

Budapest basked in the sunshine of the turn-of-the-century optimism. Within a century it had become one of the major cities of the continent. An ambitious investment of more than 300 million forints between 1874 and 1896 had completed the transformation of the modest settlement of 54,000 people into a metropolis of over 600,000, nurturing a steady climb from forty-second to tenth place among European urban populations. By the end of the century Budapest was the undisputed center of Hungarian commerce, finance, communications, and industrial development. Its carefully planned streets and parks, its imposing rows of large apartment houses and wealthy mansions, its massive railway terminals, museums, hotels, and theaters occupied the fashionable central district where elegantly attired men and women could be seen strolling and shopping.

Although somewhat marred by the noisy May Day demonstrations of thousands of workers, who were dispersed by quick and brutal police action, the millennial festivities opened with a gala performance at the National Opera, followed by a high mass in the famed Matthias Church, fireworks on Mount Gellért, overlooking the brightly lighted city, a military parade, and a glittering ball in the Royal Palace. Dressed in the uniform of a hussar general and surrounded by colorfully attired members of the nobility and purple-gowned clerical eminences who stood in conspicuous contrast to the somberly dressed Empress Elizabeth (she had worn black since the suicide of her son, Crown Prince Rudolf, in 1889), Emperor Francis Joseph was engrossed in a series of carefully arranged official functions. He made a ceremonial visit to the royal crown, which had been put on public display, laid the cornerstone for a new wing of the Royal Palace, held a reception for Hungarian and Croatian provincial governors, and reviewed a parade of troops who wore replicas of a variety of centuries—old uniforms and carried historical weapons and standards. Hundreds of thousands of enthusiastic Hungarians lined the streets and boulevards hoping to catch a glimpse of prancing horses, decorated carriages, and elegant dignitaries. Opportunities for more leisurely activities and fuller participation awaited them in the Városliget, the large park where the Millennial Exhibit was held.

No segment of the Dual Monarchy's diverse population responded to the millennial year more enthusiastically than the Hungarian Jews. Their spiritual and intellectual leaders spearheaded an outburst of communal celebration honoring Hungary's thousand-year-long national identity. The millennial year, however, was also a monument to the proud self-image of the Hungarian Jews themselves, in whom devotion to their faith and love of their nation were inextricably fused. "The words, Israelite and Magyar, have become one, constituting a sacred and symbolic unity in our consciousness," exulted Rabbi Sámuel Kohn, a prominent spiritual leader, a distinguished historian, and an indefatigable champion of assimilation. "We know that in our nation the former is as old as the latter, that of all religions practiced by its people the Jewish is the oldest, not only because it is the mother of all of them but because it is the oldest in this land and the *only one* which could celebrate with Hungary its millennial existence, for it had already been here when this land became the country of the Magyars and also accompanied those who seized this land with their blood." Similar proudly nationalistic sentiments were echoed in a lengthy, enthusiastic poem composed by Arnold Kiss, a well-known rabbi and a prolific poet, writer, and translator. "Allow not, our Lord, that 'To battle! Forward' be heard again to infinity; We are prepared to die for our country, Die to the last man!" A less euphoric and more reasoned tone was struck by Lajos Blau, professor at the prestigious National Rabbinical Seminary and a scholar of an uncommonly broad range of interests and activities. In contrast to his nostalgic, backward-gazing coreligionists he looked at the European Jewries of the modern age, welcoming the emergence of the "new Jews" and praising their manifold contributions to society. Lamenting the timidity of the Jews of old, which he attributed to the protracted state of "persecuted innocence," yet proudly recalling the high level of Jewish cultural achievements, Blau concluded that it was "this new Jewry that washed away from the name of Israel the rust of centuries." However, even his supranational vision revealed the powerful impulses of patriotism. "Among the founders of contemporary European civilization the new Jewry is coming to deserve an appropriate place in the acknowledgment of its contributions. We may be proud of this, for excepting the rebirth of the Magyar nation, no such rejuvenation, virtually overnight, of a people that had been regarded as caducous and suffering from complete exhaustion is recorded in the annals of world history."

The Jews greeted the millenial year with a meticulously orchestrated expression of communal policy, historically deep-rooted and Hungaro-centric. Even though large-scale immigration from Austria-Germany, Moravia-Bohemia, and Poland had accentuated the public image of Jews in Hungary as readily recognizable aliens who were outside the mainstream of Hungarian national consciousness, the leaders of the Jewish community, enlisting the service of Jewish scholars, consistently strove to propagate a history-conscious self-view that was as nationalistic as that of their non-Jewish countrymen. To the accustomed ingredients of Jewish life in the Diaspora—observance of religious tradition, intellectual pursuit, and economic, mostly commercial, activity—two new elements were added: chronological perspective and military posture. Authors of scholarly books and articles began to document and explain these additional elements, stressing both the vulnerability and the breadth of the Jewish-Hungarian experience. They pointed out that Jews had resided in Pannonia hundreds of years before the arrival of the wandering Magyar tribes in Dacia, Hungary's future southeastern regions, and in the northwestern lands that belonged to the domains of the Slav ruler Sviatopolk, and they cited convincing examples of archeological and written evidence. However, as the late nineteenth century was an age of turbulent nationalism and aggressive militarism, the finer points of historical chronology may have come and gone unappreciated, even unnoticed. A potentially more promising and longer lasting impression was created by other, more startling revelations: in the ninth century the Magyar tribes had been the allies of the powerful Khazars of the Crimea; Levedi, one of the early tribal leaders, had married a Jewish Khazar noblewoman; and Árpád, the paramount chief of the Magyar tribes whose descendants, the kings of the House of Árpád, were to rule Hungary for four hundred years, was elected in a ceremony the high point of which was his being raised on a shield following a Khazar custom. Perhaps an even more dramatic impact was made when it became known that Jews shared in the most sacred deed of Hungarian history: the conquest of the land that was to become the Hungarian national state. Three Judaized Khazar tribes, known as Kabars, who had left their Crimean homeland in the aftermath of a civil war, joined the Magyars as allies and fought valiantly alongside them. Amiable relations, however, could not survive the Hungarians' conversion to Christianity and the stringent anti-Jewish laws that were to keep the Jews of the land in an unyielding socioeconomic confinement for nearly nine hundred years. Not until the spirit of the Enlightenment belatedly touched Hungary's rigid class-conscious and mostly anachronistic social structure were the Jews allowed to extricate themselves from their institutionalized isolation.

At first the gestures and acts of rapprochement were almost exclusively unidirectional. A growing number of Jews made preparations to remake their image and prove their economic utility. Cautiously more and more of them followed the new though controversial course of social assimilation pioneered by German Reform Jews. The Neologs, as they were called, opened an ever-widening gap between themselves and their religiously fundamentalist and socially isolationist coreligionists, the Orthodox. They espoused a quick-paced program of reform, aimed at a radical transformation of communal character. Unmistakably clear expressions of intent, made for the benefit of Jews and non-Jews alike, were followed by determined action.

Lipót Löw (1811-75), rabbi of Szeged, one of the most distinguished and influential spiritual leaders of Hungarian Jewry, removed a major obstacle in the path of assimilation by declaring that Jewish Messianic expectations were exclusively religious in nature and that Jews were distinguishable from the peoples they lived among only in their belief and practice of their faith, thus rebutting the frequently expressed charge of the Jews' inherent inassimilability and questionable loyalty as citizens. Löw's unequivocal declaration was bolstered by the various manifestations of intense Magyarization, a process of acculturation that began in 1840 and became both in theory and practice the cornerstone of the philosophy of the Neologs. The most heartfelt expression of this communal philosophy, and a gesture that should have silenced the persistent voices of irrational criticism but did not, was the participation of Jews in the Revolution of 1848. Hundreds of Jewish volunteers fought heroically, earning praise from the commanders of the revolutionary armies as well as promotions and medals. No less impressive was the service of the noncombattants. Jewish army doctors worked valiantly, Jewish communities pledged huge sums for the purchase of hospital supplies and war materiel, and Jewish merchants played a vital role in maintaining the flow of provisions to the revolutionary forces. Even the victorious Austrians paid an inadvertent tribute in the dismal aftermath of the ill-fated revolution. They imposed a heavy fine on the Jews of Hungary for their unmistakable display of patriotism.

The post-1848 era, despite the Austrians' heavy-handed treatment of the vanquished Hungarians, witnessed no diminution of Jewish contributions in the national interest. As a belated, though not uncontested nod to Hungary's emergence from medievalism into the Industrial Age and in recognition of the many services of its Jewish minority, in December 1867 the Hungarian Diet voted to bestow on Jews equality in matters of civil liberties and political rights. It took another twenty-five years before the Diet passed a bill that recognized Judaism as an "accepted religion," placing it on an equal footing with all Christian denominations.

Thus by 1896 as Hungarians prepared to celebrate the millennium of their existence as a nation, the gulf that set Jews apart from Christians in matters of citizenship had been narrowed by legal means. Only a lingering anti-Semitism prevented it from being closed altogether. Having partially abandoned the Church-inspired stance of automatic and unquestioning hatred, and still unaffected as yet by the novel tenets of social and political demagoguery, anti-Semitism in Hungary was in an uneasy limbo, confined to a smoldering suspicion and distrust, waiting for a signal. Alternately bewildered and angered by the government's new, protective policy toward those who had for centuries been labeled "Christ-killers," most Hungarians remained oblivious to the efforts of Jews to gain social acceptance through Magyarization and increased economic usefulness. In fact, growing visibility and government-sponsored improvements in social and legal status created a popular impression of Jews as ambitious upstarts and heartless, profiteering exploiters. Few non-Jewish Hungarians cared about the historical roots of coexistence and cooperation between Jews and Hungarians.

Suddenly, albeit not unpredictably, something occurred that broke through the thin and fragile veneer of civility and exploded in a medieval spectacle that embarrassed the government and the liberal segments of the population and shocked the world. In Tiszaeszlár, a village in northeastern Hungary, a group of Jews was accused of murdering a Christian servant girl in the spring of 1882. In the course of a lengthy investigation the local authorities resorted to intimidation, humiliation, and torture and prepared for a well-publicized trial in the nearby city of Nyíregyháza.

Though the evidence presented against the defendants was contrived, having been obtained through the manipulation of unreliable witnesses, the anti-Semites wasted no time in espousing "the cause of justice" and transforming the case into a springboard for their long-awaited political counteroffensive. The trial ended in the acquittal of the accused Jews, thanks mostly to the labors of a spirited team of defense lawyers led by Károly Eötvös, a much-respected lawyer-politician. Still, it unleashed a menacing wave of anti-Semitic demonstrations across the nation and served as a convenient point of origin for Hungary's minuscule Anti-Semitic Party, founded by one of the earliest champions of political anti-Semitism in Europe, Győző Istóczy. His philosophy failed to generate a mass following, though it remained for some time, more a pesky embarrassment than a substantive issue on the political scene. The damage, however, was undeniable and could not be explained away by reassuring statements made by the government of Kálmán Tisza. Thus the modern political and racial version of the old "Jewish Question" found its niche in Hungary's political establishment.

Unlike hundreds of thousands of their coreligionists in Germany, Poland, and Russia, who in the course of the nineteenth century sought to escape the economic hardships of the post-Napoleon era and the largely uncontrolled, often spontaneous outbursts of anti-Semitic violence by emigrating to the United States, the overwhelming majority of Hungarian Jewry, both the Neologs and the Orthodox, were determined to ride out the dangerous times. Astonishingly the Neologs not only ignored the danger signals but actually redoubled their efforts to prove their socioeconomic and cultural worth and their loyalty to the nation. The forward-looking and often impulsively pragmatic government likewise preferred to act as if the "Jewish Question" did not exist, pretending that the "cultured Israelites" of Budapest, i.e., the Neologs, somehow compensated for the "kaftaned, long-sideburned" Jews of the countryside and neutralized their distinctive, thus objectionable, characteristics. However, the people remained unconvinced. Despite many arguments proving and disproving its existence, the "Jewish Question" became a permanent feature of the Hungarian landscape. Hungary's "new Jews," however, remained undaunted in the face of troubled times that would surely come. Like their ancestors in the preceding millennium, they managed to retain their identity, faith, and culture and responded quickly and with determination to the ever-widening scope of possibilities that the government-sponsored program of assimilation and modernization was offering. They became journalists, bankers, industrialists, writers, poets, artists, scholars, and—perhaps most remarkably—athletes, and excelled in their endeavors.

Any attempt to prove the participation of Hungarian Jews in sports prior to the nineteenth century will have to be made without the benefit of corroborating sources. The absence of these, however, should not rule out the prudent use of inference or circumstancial evidence. We may reasonably believe that if sports activity developed after the Church-and government-sponsored restrictions were removed and the enforced confinement of Jews was lifted, it could also have developed before those restrictions and confinement were imposed. Thus similar conditions at the two extremities of the Hungarians' millennial national experience may have produced similar occurrences.

In the first chapter of *A magyar testnevelés és sport története* [History of Hungarian physical education and sport], a multiauthored work, the Jewish Éva Földes, one of the most prominent contemporary Hungarian sport historians and the bronze medal winner in literature at the 1948 London Olympic Games, describes the training of Magyar youths in riding, swimming, throwing, and archery, as well as the maneuvers of the strong-bodied Magyar warriors to which the ninth-century Byzantine emperor Leo the Wise was an appreciative witness and chronicler. Preoccupation with warfare perpetuated the tradition of militarism that remained the most characteristic feature of Magyar life at the threshold of the conquest and thereafter.

The impression of physical strength the Magyars generated cannot have gone unnoticed by the three Jewish Khazar tribes, the Kabars, who had joined them as allies and took part in the conquest. That the Kabars were no mere tagalongs is a matter of record. The Magyars respected the Kabars' warlike qualities and allowed them to act as a vanguard. For some time after the conquest the Magyars even spoke the Khazar language in addition to their own. Though the Kabars may not be said to have belonged to the mainstream of Judaism—there are few references to them in the works of medieval Jewish authors—in the eyes of the pagan Magyars the even superficially Judaized Kabars must have appeared as fearsome worshippers of an awe-inspiring, unseen God. The subsequent establishment of the Magyars' national state and their conversion to Christianity drove a wedge between the allies. The corresponding decrease in respect for the Jewish Kabars among the Christian Magyars and the ensuing tradition of anti-Jewish legislation helped weaken the once-commanding image of the Kabars. Their reputation for physical prowess and military skills faded. The emergent popular image of the Jew was that of a suspicious and un-healthy-looking religious infidel whose only redeeming quality was his eco-nomic worth as a merchant, money lender, estate steward, and tax col-lector—a far cry from the warlike figure of the hard-fighting Kabar.

The age of restriction, discrimination, and prejudice proved to be un-yielding and long-lasting. It pushed the Jews beyond the pale of Hungarian society. They were timid onlookers of the Christian Hungarians' growing infatuation with the knightly combat of medieval chivalry and the militant service of God and king. The protracted confinement to the sidelines of Hungarian life bred generations of Jews who held physical prowess in low esteem, instead turning to religion and scholarship as the proper life for a Jew.

Ironically, the famous statue of Miklós Toldi, the immensely powerful fourteenth-century warrior-knight whom folk legend and epic transformed into the quintessential Magyar hero, was modeled after Dávid Müller, the outstanding Jewish gymnast of the late 1880s, who was said to have been the most beautifully muscled Magyar of his time. No less remarkable is the fact that Botond, the legendary hero of the Magyars' attack on Con-stantinople, who smashed his axe into the gate of the city and who wrestled a giant Greek to the ground, found his twentieth-century counterpart in the Jewish Richárd Weisz. Of Weisz's strength numerous stories, both real and fabricated, were told. He became Hungary's first Olympic champion, winning the gold medal in the heavyweight division at the 1908 London Olympics.

Still, a number of puzzling details of the Jewish experience in medieval Hungary emerge. In 1476 a delegation of 200 Jews wearing prayer shawls solemnly followed a group of 26 prominent members of the Jewish com-munity, dressed in festive garments, with ostrich feathers stuck in their hats and on horseback, at the head of which the president and his son rode with unsheathed swords. It was part of the procession that greeted King Matthias and his bride. In an age when Jews in most European countries were forced to wear the humiliating Jewish badge on their outer garments and distinctive hats and were forbidden to bear arms, the spectacle of that delegation presented an intriguing exception to the accustomed visual image of Jews. Nor did the protracted age of discrimination and persecution extirpate the fighting spirit of the Jews. During the century-and-half-long Turkish occupation of Hungary (1526-1699) the Jews were treated like loyal, trusted, and useful subjects, which they were, and they responded in kind. They fought desperately alongside the Turkish defenders of Buda, suffering high casualties as the victorious Austrians killed many survivors of the siege. Similar manifestations of the Jews' willingness to fight in the bloody battles of the 1848 Revolution and the First World War would become a matter of record and a source of communal pride.

Surprisingly, the entry of Hungarian Jews into sports came much later than the beginning of their participation in professions from which they had been barred by law and the vestiges of discriminatory medieval Christian guild practices. One of the principal reasons for the delay was the prevailing pedagogical philosophy. Although the *Ratio educationis* of 1777 —the first attempt of the state to regulate public education—ordered compulsory physical education for school children so that they might become healthy citizens and able-bodied soldiers, the *Ratio educationis* of 1806 reversed the promising trend and returned physical education to the home and the discretion of the parents. Not until 1868 was physical education remanded to the lower levels of the public school system, whose curriculum planners assigned two hours per week to *testgyakorlás* ["physical culture"]. By the early 1870s many Jewish parents had enrolled their children in public schools. Thus it is safe to assume that they had no objection to the children's participation in physical education classes, which then consisted of free exercises, marching and tumbling in groups, and some games. However, physical education did not become compulsory in the high schools until 1883. Even then most educators grumbled about all that "useless marching" and "military training." Since more Jewish students attended public high school than elementary and middle school (there already were schools run by the Jewish community on the lower level but not the higher) the number of Jewish students who had been deprived of participation in what would incontestably become the most popular part of the curriculum was greater than the number of those who were exposed to it. At this time, a scant thirteen years before the first modern Olympic Games were to take place, Jewish school children were still only standing at the threshold of physical education. The first steps they would take quickly turned into giant strides.

The second reason for the Jews' delayed entry into sports was the ambivalent attitude of three of Hungary's most respected politicians, Baron Miklós Wesselényi, Lajos Kossuth, and Count István Széchenyi. These men happened to be the principal supporters of the creation of an intellectually and physically progressive educational system as well as enthusiastic participants in sporting activity. Lacking sufficient knowledge of the distinctive features of Diaspora Judaism or perhaps unduly influenced by the exclusiveness of the Orthodox, none of the three could imagine that of the various ethnic groups—Jews, Greeks, Serbs, and Armenians—the Jews would be the quickest and most enthusiastic in espousing the tenets of liberal nationalism. Within a generation, however, the burgeoning assimilation and Magyarization of the Neologs would prove all three wrong. Still, these architects of Hungarian sport could not have relied then on the segment of the population that would ultimately become one of its pillars. The foundations of target shooting, horseback riding, rowing, running, swimming, fencing, and gymnastics were laid down in the 1820s and 1830s, a decade before the quick-paced Magyarization of the Neologs began.

Surprisingly, the clairvoyance that Wesselényi, Széchenyi and Kossuth displayed in matters of national politics was absent in their efforts to introduce sports in Hungary. Wesselényi and Széchenyi in particular wrote clearly and persuasively of the importance of exposing Hungarian youth to physical education and served as models by personal example. The robust Wesselényi was an accomplished target shooter, equestrian, fencer, and swimmer, and Széchenyi excelled in swimming and rowing. Yet it occurred to neither that Jews and sports were not mutually exclusive and that young Jews, given the opportunity to participate in a progressive educational environment, could achieve results that compared favorably to and even exceeded those of their non-Jewish counterparts.

In 1822 both Wesselényi and Széchenyi visited England and were introduced to boxing. Wesselényi, the more physically agile and adventurous of the two, actually received instruction from two famous champions, John Jackson and Tom Spring. Széchenyi was so determined to popularize boxing in Hungary that he even coined the word öklész, the earliest word for "pugilist." It is surprising that in view of their enthusiasm for the sport, neither man should have heard of the Jewish David Mendoza, who became champion of England in 1792 and was the father of scientific boxing. They were equally oblivious to the other well-known Jewish pugilists of the late eighteenth and early nineteenth century, such as Barney Aaron, the "Star of the East," Solomon Sodickey, Isaac Bitoon, Samuel Elias, and other bare-knuckle fighters. One is tempted to speculate what Wesselényi and Széchenyi might have said had someone suggested to them that the first Hungarian Olympic champions in fencing and swimming, two of their favorite sports, would be Jews.

No documentary evidence may be cited to prove the participation of Jews in sports or their membership in the early sport clubs that came into being in the 1820s and 1830s, largely at the initiative of Wesselényi, Széchenyi, and Kossuth. Nor did the aftermath of the 1848 Revolution and the Emancipation of Hungarian Jewry in 1867 produce substantive changes for the better. The sport clubs provided opportunities for adventurous individuals to step over social boundaries and band together with other devotees of their sport. The Budapesti Hajósegylet ("Boating Club of Budapest"), the nation's first gathering place of rowing enthusiasts, was founded in April 1861 by a group of liberal aristocrats who invited interested members of the increasingly wealthy and socially prominent *haut-bourgeois* families to join the club. Social intermingling, however, did not lead to the removal of religious barriers. Even though by the early 1860s a number of Jewish families such as the Goldbergers, Fischers, and Neuschlosses, manufacturers of textiles, porcelain wares, and wood products, respectively, had become wealthy and prominent, the club's membership roster listed only two identifiably Jewish names, Koppely and Wodianer, whose bearers, however, were converted to Catholicism.

A change in national leadership that brought Ferenc Deák, Baron József Eötvös, and Kálmán Tisza to political prominence bred a new, pragmatic attitude toward Jews, recognizing their potential for making manifold contributions to Hungary's capitalist society and the possibilities of cooperation with the assimilationist community leaders. In the long run, the most tangible and progressive results grew out of the close association of Eötvös and Ignác Hirschler. Since the late 1850s Eötvös had been an exponent of physical education and a firm believer in the indispensable utility of an assimilated and Magyarized Jewry, while Hirschler, the president of Budapest's Neolog community, was a loyal supporter of Eötvös's philosophy and program of sweeping reforms. Relations between the government and the Jewish community had at long last advanced beyond the enduring tradition of mutual suspicion and animosity and now rested on the firmer foundation of mutual respect.

Still the actual start of the Jews' entry into the realm of sports remains elusive. The data are inferential rather than evidentiary. As Pál Fábián, author of the entry "Sport" in the *Magyar zsidó lexikon,* rightly observed, "Only in the field of sport was religious affiliation not taken into account." However, the entry "Athletics," which was also contributed by Fábián, is a repository of a wide range of outstanding achievements in competition for national championships. The last generation before the First World War produced an impressive list of Jewish champions. The surprising and unexpected consequence of the Jews' entry into sports was in contrast to all other avenues of Jewish assimilationism, including the military, in which the theoretical brotherhood of the wounded and dead should have obviated the identification of religious origin, the appearance of Jewish athletes and the news of their outstanding achievements elicited hardly any comments from those who objected to the rapidity and extent of the assimilation of the Jews. Ironically, of all versions of social interaction only sport was exempted from the increasingly popular game, played with enthusiasm by Jews and non-Jews alike, of identifying the religion of anyone seen, read, or spoken about. The Jew-baiters felt that their traditional arguments, based on the fundamental unassimilability of Jews, would have been deprived of even the faintest ring of credibility if directed against powerful figures whose very physical appearance, notwithstanding their Jewishness, was an inspiring reminder of the qualities such as bravery and determination which Hungarians claimed were the essence of their millennial national existence. Surprisingly, the Jews did not seem to be eager to make an issue of it. The road to assimilation would have to bypass the sensitivities of non-Jewish Hungarians. Circumvention rather than head-on confrontation was thought the better strategy for achieving public acceptance.

CHAPTER II

THE FIRST GENERATION OF JEWISH CHAMPIONS

To the overwhelming majority of late nineteenth-century Hungarians, Jews were the very antitheses of the values, traditions, self-image, and physical appearance which were associated with the Hungarians' millennial national past and which they wished to preserve. Jews could offer no communal or individual contribution that would be accepted as evidence of genuine assimilation. But if neither the liberal politicians' statements of praise nor the government's patronage of Magyarization had the slightest effect on the public's view of Jews or acted to retard the slowly regrouping forces of anti-Semitism, few Jews were willing to admit it. The wave of unjust accusations after the ill-fated 1848 Revolution, the passionate arguments against the Emancipation, the mass hysteria that accompanied the tragic case of Tiszaeszlár, and the advent of political anti-Semitism were all too obvious danger signals. Yet they were misinterpreted or ignored by those to whom they should have become a sobering warning. One should not seek permanent refuge in a house of cards.

Still, if fin-de-siècle Hungary was a shaky edifice, it was not without attractive features. Few onlookers realized that, however inviting, a superstructure resting on weak foundations would only temporarily conceal its precarious vulnerability. By the time the millennial year of 1896 arrived, their contributions to Hungary's modernization had become for Jews a source of communal pride, the basis of social and financial gain for many, and the springboard to ennoblement for a few; for the government

14

they yielded substantial returns on a practical, albeit unpopular, investment. The first waves of political anti-Semitism, which caused embarrassment to the government and apprehension among the Jews, had dissipated
by then. The euphoria that the millennial celebrations touched off seemed
to cast a veil over the inequalities and unjustices of the past and the ugly
manifestations of popular hatred. As Hungarians strove to outdo one another in the noisy display of patriotic fervor, the Jews were preparing to
make contributions of a new kind.

In the 1895 edition of the *Évkönyv* [Yearbook] of the Izraelita Magyar
Irodalmi Társulat ("Hungarian Jewish Literary Association"), a brief
article will inevitably strike the reader as being strangely out of tune with
the general tone and topical range. Nestled between a lengthy, teary poem
about a visit to the cemetery and a short story portraying Jewish life in
the countryside, "A testi nevelés és a zsidóság" [Physical Education and
Jewry] presents a remarkably cogent argument in favor of the least cultivated aspect of assimilation. Its author, Dr. Henrik Schuschny (1857-
1929), was a respected physician and lecturer. Schuschny's presentation
is straightforward, his reasoning unassailable. Jewish assimilation to Hungarian society, he noted, despite many undoubtedly successful attempts
and noteworthy achievements in times of war and peace, was incomplete.
Physical education, which Jews had traditionally neglected, would lead
to the removal of the last obstacles and complete the process of assimilation. "If systematically taught and practised, physical education will
increase not only physical strength but also self-confidence and self-
respect," Schuschny concluded. "When in addition to patriotism and culture the Hungarian Jew has acquired a healthy and trained body and
self-respect, the only difference between him and the other patriotic
citizens of the country will be religion . . . . At the threshold of the celebration of the millennial existence of the Hungarian nation and at the start
of the new millennium, let us think of these things, too. Our country may
need courageous men, our society will always depend on healthy citizens.
Let us fulfill our obligations in this respect, as well."

Schuschny's article was a landmark in the multidimentional process of
Jewish assimilation. Indeed, all approaches had been tried, all avenues
explored. All except one. In a country where strength, skill, and agility
had been the most easily discernible features of national tradition and
pride, no segment of the population could keep aloof from physical

culture without paying the penalty. Schuschny's observations cast light on two significant objectives—one implicit, the other easily recognizable—that had already been achieved. He refrained from advancing his arguments in the technical language of physiology and instead presented a simple, albeit inspired spectacle of psychological and physical benefits with which a healthy and robust Jewry would gain the complete acceptance of Hungarian society. By allowing the article to appear in its most influential journal, the leadership of the Jewish community was officially endorsing Schuschny's views.

Schuschny's vision was overshadowed by the achievements of Baron Pierre de Coubertin and the athletes who as Olympic champions have become national heroes. His name is unfamiliar even to Hungarians, who are second to none in the love of sport and can virtually recite by heart the names of the more than a hundred Olympic gold medal winners their country has produced. Yet without Schuschny's enthusiasm, Hungary might not have even been a participant in the first modern Olymic Games.

Schuschny's pioneering effort to propagate the national benefits of physical education was carried a step further by Ferenc Kemény (1860-1944). The son of Jewish parents in Nagybecskerek, now a part of Yugoslavia but then a city in southern Hungary, Kemény was educated in Budapest and Paris. Upon receiving his diploma he taught in a number of provincial cities before he was appointed to a school in Budapest. A prolific writer, his articles on pedagogy appeared in Hungarian, English, and French journals. He was also the author of a number of scholarly books, in addition to being the secretary of the peace movement in Hungary.

Formidably mustachioed and meticulously attired, Kemény looked more like an exponent of the soldierly virtues than a gentle pedagogue and a lifelong pacifist. That he should become an instant convert to the Olympic idea—he had personally known Coubertin since their student days in Paris and shared his intellectual outlook—was perhaps a predictable consequence of his profession and convictions. However, for a Jew professing an unshakable faith in the brotherhood of man and peaceful coexistence to have been allowed to represent Hungary, the militant "Bastion of Christianity," in the incipient Olympic movement was surely one of the more surprising twists of fate even in that paradox-rich nation. Moreover, that a Jew should become the first Hungarian member of the International Olympic Committee must have been a source of pride to the Jewish community.

To those who are accustomed to the sounds and sights of sports, Greece and the Olympic Games go hand in hand. It may come as somewhat of a surprise that a slight alteration of timing and circumstances might have made Budapest, not Athens, the gathering place of the small group of organizers who were to help make a dream become reality. Coubertin's passionate vision and unabating efforts nearly foundered, at least temporarily, due to the unforeseen difficulties which the last stages of planning presented. Though the tradition-conscious Greeks were elated at the prospect of hosting the reemergence of one of the most hallowed institutions of their ancestors, the Greek government, citing financial problems, delayed the start of the preparations. Suddenly the Hungarians came up with an intriguing proposal. In October 1894 Kemény and Count Albin Csáky, a former minister of culture, informed Coubertin that in view of the predicament of the Greek government, Budapest might be considered as an alternative to Athens. The Hungarian offer, however, may have only been a cleverly disguised ploy. Kemény probably knew that Coubertin would not agree to changing the location of the Games, but the prospect of even a remote possibility that Athens would not be the city which sportsfans of all future generations would identify with the rebirth of the Olympic Games was enough to prompt the Greek government to abandon its wait-and-see attitude and lunge into a quick-paced activity to complete the preparations. Preoccupied with its own mounting concerns in connection with the millennial celebrations, the government of Hungary showed no enthusiasm for hosting the Games. Had it not been for the millennium, however, things might have turned out differently.

Later generations of Hungarians for whom the enthusiastic support of their Olympic athletes became a national tradition may have found it difficult to believe that in the beginning few people cared if Hungary would be a participant or not. The government was exceedingly thrifty in allocating funds. Its paltry contribution of a thousand forints had to be augmented by lesser sums pledged by four sport clubs. On 10 March 1896, only eight days before the first of two groups of Olympians were scheduled to leave by train for Athens, the Hungarian Olympic Committee met to select by secret ballot the members of Hungary's first Olympic team. It is interesting to note that of the seven selected, three—Alfréd Hajós-Guttmann, Gyula Kellner, and Dezső Wein—were Jews. The first two of these received the highest number of votes: fourteen members had voted for Hajós-Guttmann, thirteen for Kellner.

It was a strange-looking, modestly small team—seven competitors and six officials and technical personnel. It aroused no nationwide interest, let alone support. Kornél Őszi, the Jewish editor of *Sportélet* [Sporting Life], observed in the first edition of the newspaper (15 March 1896), "I greatly fear that the competitors in Athens will be Hungarians in mourning. They will return soundly beaten and utterly failed. I don't want to say that they shouldn't go; rather I suggest they go to Athens and see by how much the foreigners are ahead of us."

Still, Hungary was one of the twelve nations—the Greek government had sent invitations to thirty-six—that participated in the first Olympic Games of modern times. The Hungarian nation would be indebted to a large extent to its Jewish athletes for its success in Athens.

Alfréd Hajós-Guttmann (1878-1955) was Hungary's Renaissance man of sports. Born in Budapest, Hajós-Guttmann was in many ways the typical product of the increasingly secularized environment that the assimilationist Jews had created. Although he was only thirteen when he lost his father—it was one of the tragic ironies of fate that the son of the man who drowned in the Danube would grow up to be his country's first internationally famous swimming champion—Hajós-Guttmann suffered few of the effects that often accompany the sudden death of a parent. He was a well-adjusted young man, physically and intellectually, largely due to his hard-working mother, who took great care in the upbringing of her five children. He had already been swimming competitively for some years. In 1895 he won a European championship in Vienna, having made the journey sitting on the wooden bench of a train and sustained by a gift of twenty forints from friends and relatives. He spent long hours in training to develop a smooth style. Although the standard technique at the time was to kick like a frog, he preferred to use his legs mostly for balance and propelled himself almost exclusively with his arms. Upon finishing his high school studies, Hajós-Guttmann enrolled in the School of Architecture at the University of Budapest. Notwithstanding one of his professor's firm conviction that "only lazy people engage in sport . . . . Drinking, playing cards, dancing, and sport lead to nothing good," he proved to be both a good and diligent student and a champion swimmer.

On 30 March 1896 a crowd of 40,000 watched the competition for Olympic medals in the four swimming events that took place in chilly waters of the Bay of Piraeus. Swimming furiously and looking neither right or left, Hajós-Guttmann battled the waves. He reached the finish first among the twenty competitors in the 100-meter event with a time of 1:22.2, thereby becoming Hungary's first Olympic champion. The low temperature of the water cost him an event, however. He had intended to swim in the 500-meter competition as well, but was advised against doing so, on the grounds of exhaustion. He consented to sit out the race, but after an hour and a half of invigorating massage, he was ready for further competition. His body covered with a heavy layer of grease for protection, Hajós-Guttmann, one of the thirty-one competitors in the 1200 meters, plunged into the water. His performance was a remarkable exhibition of courage, endurance, and talent. While some exhausted swimmers had to be pulled out of the water into the accompanying boats, Hajós-Guttmann continued to dictate a furious pace. The Hungarian flag went up before he even reached the finish. The "Hungarian dolphin," the name the admiring Greek newspapers bestowed upon him, won his second Olympic championship with the time of 18:22.2, fifteen meters ahead of the Greek Andreu.

Hajós-Guttmann's Olympic performance has generally been thought to have overshadowed his nonswimming achievements. He was a talented soccer player and a member of Hungary's first national soccer team, twice selected to represent his country in international matches. He was an expert gymnast and competed in the colors of the Gymnastics Club of Budapest. He also excelled in discus throwing, boxing, and running the 100-meter dash. He retired from competition in 1904 but remained interested in sports. His advice was eagerly sought to the end of his life. Finally, Hajós-Guttmann was a talented and highly respected architect. His stadium plans, submitted jointly with Dezső Lauber, another Jewish architect, earned the silver medal—the gold was not awarded—in architecture at the 1924 Paris Olympics. Hajós-Guttmann designed Budapest's famed Nemzeti Sportuszoda ("National sport swimming pool") and participated in the remodeling of Császár fürdő, another swimming facility built over Roman mineral wells, and the Millenáris sport complex.

In the light of Hajós-Guttmann's two Olympic gold medals the performance of the other Hungarian-Jewish Olympians is understandably dimmed. Gyula Kellner, a powerfully built and serious-looking long-distance runner, was awarded the bronze medal in the marathon run. The winner, provided he was a Greek and a Christian, was awarded prizes ranging from a dowry of a million drachmas and the hand of the daughter of George Averoff, the principal financial backer of the Games, to free lifetime tailoring and barbering services. The marathon seemed to be the real star of the Olympics, virtually overshadowing even the runners. Twenty-one of the twenty-five runners were Greek. Of the four non-Greeks, only Kellner had any experience in running such a distance. The Australian Edwin Flack, winner of the 100-meter and 1500-meter races, the American Arthur Blake, and the Frenchman L. Lermusiaux, who finished second and third in the 1500-meters respectively, were the other non-Greeks. Predictably, the Greeks dominated the event and ultimately captured first, second, third, fifth, and sixth places. However, the third-place finisher, a certain Velokas, was disqualified for having covered part of the distance on the top of a wagon. The bronze medal, as well as a gold watch presented by Prince George of Greece as a gesture of appeasement, was given to Kellner. It is interesting to note that despite his contrived mode of locomotion Velokas's time was 3:06.30, only five-tenths of a second faster than law-abiding Kellner's. Dezső Wein was the only Jewish member of the team who did not win a medal. The final tally gave Hungary sixth place, following the United States, Greece, Germany, France, and Great Britain, in the unofficial ranking.

As Ferenc Mező, the doyen of Hungarian sport historians pointed out, if the government had been more generous with its financial support of the Olympic effort, Hungary could have boasted of even more medals. Instead, its contribution was the negligible sum of 1000 forints, whereas the round-trip transportation alone for one Olympian from Budapest to Athens cost nearly 300. The Jewish athletes who might have competed with a good chance of winning medals were: Gyula Dezsényi-Deutsch, a long-distance swimmer, who in 1895 won the one-mile event in the Austrian championship; the sprinter Ármin Villányi-Weisz, who in 1895 ran the 100 meters in 11 seconds, a second faster than the time with which the American Thomas Burke would win the event in Athens; and Dávid Müller, the best Hungarian gymnast of his time. The financial limitations and the distraction due to the preparations for the millennial year notwithstanding, Hungary established its position in international sports as firmly as Jewish athletes did in Hungary.

In light of Hajós-Guttmann's and Kellner's achievements in 1896, expectations of continued good performance by Jewish athletes were well founded. Surprisingly, neither of the next two Olympic Games justified such expectations. The Olympic teams that represented Hungary in Paris (1900) and St. Louis (1904) included no Jewish athletes. However, the absence of Jewish Olympians did not mean the absence of Jews from the Olympic effort. Two Jews made significant contributions in noncompetitive capacities to the country's Olympic performance. Ferenc Kemény was one of the leaders of the Hungarian teams that participated in the Paris and St. Louis Olympics and continued his labors on behalf of the International Olympic Committee. And Alfréd Brüll supported the Hungarian sports effort in countless ways.

Brüll (1876-1944), one of Hungary's most generous patrons of sports and athletes, was the behind-the-scenes counterpart of Hajós-Guttmann in the variety of his talents and the excellence of his achievements. A wealthy philanthropist who moved with equal facility in the world of high finance, the circles of the socially and cerebrally privileged, and the locker rooms of Hungarian sport, Brüll in 1905 became president of the *MTK* (Magyar Testnevelők Köre), one of Hungary's most famous sport clubs, to which the majority of Jewish athletes belonged at one time or another and with which his name was synonymous for the next few decades. Brüll's knowledge of foreign languages and proficiency in public speaking soon catapulted him into the world of national and international sports. In the course of his distinguished career, the magnitude of which is yet to be acknowledged by contemporary Hungarian sport historians, Brüll served as an Olympic swimming and gymnastics official (1906-08), first vice-president of the Hungarian Athletic Association (1904), president of the Hungarian Swimming Association, vice-president of the Hungarian Gymnastics Association (1908), president of the Hungarian Wrestling Association (1921), and president of the World Wrestling League (1924). He was also a founding member of the Hungarian Soccer Association (1906). It was Brüll's unquestioning generosity that enabled Géza Kiss, a talented long-distance swimmer who had transferred to the *MTK*, to attend the 1904 Olympic Games in St. Louis, where he won the silver medal in the one-mile freestyle event and the bronze in the half-mile.

The absence of contributions by Jewish athletes to the Hungarians' Olympic efforts in 1900 and 1904 was more than amply made up in later years. Indeed Hungary's path to Olympic fame in the 1908 Olympic Games in London, especially its quest for gold medals, was highlighted by the achievements of Jewish competitors. Only one event, unexpected and disturbing, cast a shadow on the otherwise auspicious pre-Olympic circumstances. Ferenc Kemény, who had been Hungary's indefatigable Olympic organizer and its representative on the International Olympic Committee, resigned after a series of acrimonious meetings with the leaders of the *MAC* (Magyar Atlétikai Club). They had been trying to acquire a decisive influence in matters relating to Olympic preparations and to the Hungarian Olympic Committee. They favored Hungary's participation in the Hellenic Games of 1906, which Kemény had opposed. The leadership of the sixty-member Hungarian Olympic team was eventually entrusted to Alfréd Brüll.

No Hungarian Olympian had succeeded in winning a medal either in fencing or wrestling, two events in which athletic, Christian, and nationalist virtues coalesced. Now, however, the heirs to Botond and Toldi had been found. Thrust into the full light of Olympic glory, accompanied by the sounds of the Hungarian national anthem and the raising of Hungary's flag of red, white, and green, two champions stood proudly as they received the gold medals. One man's name was Weisz, the other's Fuchs. Both were Jewish.

In the general mood of jubilation the irony of the moment was undoubtedly lost. Most Hungarians, Jews and non-Jews alike, were probably glad to observe one of the few exceptions to the rule that identified individuals and their achievements by religious affiliation. Christians were spared the embarrassment of having to acknowledge that two members of the traditionally hated and despised minority in their midst had excelled in the exercise of virtues that were held to be Christian; Jews would not have to be compelled to explain away yet another puzzling feature of their assimilation. Still, in view of the millennial tribulations of Hungarian Jewry and the enduring tradition of institutionalized hatred both sides were probably hard-put to keep their feelings within the bounds of civility, one suppressing the urge to gloat or at least to smirk, the other to feel resentment and bitterness.

At first glance the observer is struck by the remarkable polarity between two manifestations of physical appearance. The winner of the Olympic heavyweight championship in Greco-Roman wrestling was a man of mind-boggling physique whose image seems to be too large to be captured by camera. The winner of the Olympic saber championship was small-statured, balding, and bespectacled. In a well-known photograph, it is only the white fencing uniform and the grip of the saber that lend him an air of athletic credibility.

Richárd Weisz (1879-1945) was born in Budapest and spent his entire athletic career as a member of the *MTK*. A man of enormous strength and few words, Weisz trained hard and long. He regularly demolished his opponents with a formidable display of strength and great technical skill, though it is said that he was a worrier and a slow starter. Hugó Payr, a fellow club member, was the only Hungarian wrestler to defeat him in a Budapest championship in February 1908. He was a six-time national champion in heavyweight wrestling, from 1904-1909, and also won the middleweight title in 1903, the first in both categories in the history of that sport in Hungary. Although he professed to have only a casual interest in it—he trained a mere three weeks for the first national championship—Weisz won the first seven heavyweight titles in weightlifting. In the course of one championship, it is recalled, he bettered the national record eleven times, breaking the world record at the same time. Interestingly, Weisz had started out as a gymnast and later branched out into track and field events. He excelled in shot put, discus and hammer throwing, in high and long jumps, activities not commonly engaged in by men of his bulk.

Everybody's favorite, Weisz was destined to become the frequent subject of seemingly incredible stories, some real others probably fabricated. Once, it is told, he and Brüll, the president of the *MTK* and Weisz's friend and mentor, were walking after dark when suddenly two thugs jumped in front of them and demanded money. With the speed of lightning, Weisz threw his fists left and right, sending the thugs to the ground unconscious. The two walked on unfazed. On their way back they again came upon the thugs, still dazed by Weisz's punches. Upon Brüll's urging, Weisz gave them a quick massage, helped them to regain consciousness, and good-naturedly sent them on their way.

Another time Weisz and Brüll, so the story goes, were sitting in a sidewalk café. A man started making disparaging remarks about the two *MTK* members. Weisz stood up, stepped to the man's table and inquired if he wanted anything. "Yes," the man replied defiantly and pulled out a business card, the customary gesture of issuing a challenge to a duel. Slowly Weisz walked back to his table. With one quick and powerful yank, he tore off a corner of the marble tabletop, scribbled his name on it and had a waiter carry it to his challenger. Ashen faced, the man rose and quietly left the scene of his humiliation.

In the heat of the July sun the world's best heavyweight wrestlers were assembled on the open field of London's Olympic stadium. Weisz proved unbeatable. He pinned the Danish C. W. Jensen in 13:20. He then won on points against the taller and heavier S. Jensen, brother of his first opponent, who had won the heavyweight title at the 1906 Hellenic Games in Athens, in a twenty-minute-long match that often resembled a brawl. In the final Weisz met the immensely powerful Russian A. Petrov. The Hungarian attacked from the start and in the fifteenth minute succeeded in throwing the Russian on the mat, but could pin him only out of bounds. After an hour-long struggle—the judges extended the twenty-minute regulation time by three overtime periods of ten, twenty, and ten minutes—Weisz was declared the winner and became Hungary's first Olympic wrestling champion.

The Olympic euphoria, however, proved short-lived. Though Weisz predictably won the heavyweight national titles in weightlifting in 1908 and in wrestling in 1909, a foolish incident led to the untimely and abrupt end of his brilliant career. In those days men of great physical strength often attempted feats for money or engaged in challenge matches for bets. In the course of a training session Weisz wrestled with the visiting professional world champion Cziganiewitz. The news of the illegal bout between the amateur and the professional got out, and the Hungarian Athletic Association, in whose jurisdiction wrestling belonged, lifted Weisz's amateur license and declared him a professional. In 1912 he was pardoned and reclassified as an amateur, but when members of the Hungarian Olympic Committee eagerly sought his participation in the Stockholm Olympic Games, the disillusioned Weisz, who had given up training regularly, declined the invitation. He would wrestle no more. For the next three and a half decades Weisz found peace and happiness in the *MTK*, the club with which his name became synonymous. Indeed, except for brief periods in his youth—after graduating from a technical school he worked in the iron trade, later volunteering for a one-year stint in the Navy, and eventually becoming a bouncer in the "Nyugat," a bar owned by his family—Weisz was the quintessential clubman. He and Brüll, the wealthy and respected president of the *MTK*, were lifelong friends. After he won the Olympic championship, Weisz received a loan of 80,000 crowns from Brüll with which he purchased the "Japan," one of Budapest's trendier coffeehouses. However, even as an owner he was a bouncer at heart. Gentlemen unable to pay their bills due to temporary shortages of funds were thrown out of the "Japan" into the street as unceremoniously as the drunken and frequently brawling truckdrivers of the "Nyugat." Small wonder that the patrons of the "Japan," sensitive and unforgiving, did not appreciate their host's prowess. The evicted truckdrivers, on the other hand, were prone to boast of having survived a couple of Weisz's punches. He sold the "Japan" and repaid Brüll the loan.

He spent the rest of his life as the "emperor" of the *MTK*, lending the club prestige with his mere presence and coaching generations of young wrestlers. At last, however, the growing insanity of Hungary's interwar politics and the virulent anti-Jewish manifestations of the war years, which culminated in the brutal concluding months of the Fascist Arrow Cross era, caught up with Weisz too. Even though he had been one of the privileged members of society, he shared the ghettoization of his coreligionists. However, he never became one of the terrible statistics of the Final Solution.

Perhaps it was only too fitting that the last months of his life would be filled with preparations for the revival of the *MTK*. The first meeting of the organizing committee, of which he was a member, was held in his apartment early in February 1945 while Soviet troops were still engaged in bloody street-to-street fighting with the retreating Germans and their Arrow Cross allies. Weisz died in December 1945. Only then did it come to light that he had been named the principal beneficiary of Brüll's will. It was a touching tribute to a great sportsman by the president of the *MTK*, himself a victim of the Holocaust. When they were young men and inseparable friends Weisz was Brüll's protector; in old age the roles were reversed. Their friendship formed the firm and durable foundation of two of the most interdependent careers in the history of Hungarian sport.

Hungarian sport historians invariably take a deep breath before plunging into the description of the development of fencing. The sport began in the "Cradle of Civilization," the ancient Near East, where Egyptians, Assyrians, and Persians provided the first instances of fencing. From the deadly games of Roman gladiators through the chivalry of medieval knights to the bloody battles fought by the armies of nation states the sword has been a constant. A badge of nobility and courage, it had to be handled with skill. Countless generations of masters transmitted the art of fencing to men of high birth, who put it to good use in pursuing elegant forms of entertainment. Other fencers were seekers of fame and fortune who were habitual participants in duels and tournaments.

In Hungary too the list of men who displayed fencing skills and posed for their portraits with swords reads like a *Who's Who* in national history. The introduction of modern competition fencing is attributed to the initiatives of the two great nineteenth-century statesmen, Széchenyi and Wesselényi. The earliest and best-known masters were foreigners: the Prussian Friedrich, the French Chappon and Clair, and the Italian Biasini. From the 1850s Hungarian masters such as József Keresztessy and his son Sándor, Count Lajos Váry, and Mihály Bély took over. Still, no Hungarian fencer competed in Paris and St. Louis, the first two modern Olympic Games to feature the three events—foil, épée, and saber—that make up the fencing competition.

Notwithstanding the biblical accounts of the military exploits of the ancient Hebrews, the desperate acts of heroism against the Greek and Roman masters of Palestine, or the rare incidents of Jewish contributions to the military history of medieval Islam, the nineteen-century-long enforced powerlessness prohibited Jews of the Diaspora from bearing arms and left them without even the means of self-defense. Not even the steadily widening scope of Jewish activities in the post-Emancipation era prevents the historian from observing with disbelief the spectacle of sudden achievements that unfolded during the fencing competition at the 1908 Olympic Games. Not because the Hungarians broke into that sport which in Paris had been dominated by the French and in St. Louis by Americans and Cubans—it was not beyond the realm of possibility that representatives of this "nation of fencers" would rise to the top sooner or later—but because Hungary's first Olympic champions in fencing were Jews.

It has been suggested that fencing became popular among Jewish university students as a means of offering an effective response when challenged by anti-Semitic classmates. It may have been true of Jewish students in Hungary, too. During the infamous Tiszaeszlár affair of the early 1880s, university students participated in anti-Jewish demonstrations and were among the most enthusiastic supporters of Győző Istóczy, the founder of political anti-Semitism in Hungary. Another powerful stimulus was certainly one of the so-called national vices in late nineteenth-century Hungary: dueling. Due to the romantic image of dueling bravos and the fascination with elegantly attired gentlemen somberly making arrangements for the resolution of a formal challenge in dimly-lit rooms of coffeehouses and casinos, dueling attracted men from all walks of life. The causes ranged from rivalry for the favors of a lady to the avenging of offensive remarks, made orally or in print. Interestingly, in two of the most celebrated duels one of the participants was a Jew. Dr. Gyula Rosenberg shot Count István Batthány to death. The Hungarian nobleman wanted to marry Rosenberg's wife, the former Ilona Tornyai-Schossberger, the daughter of one of the wealthiest Jews in Hungary, whom Rosenberg had married against her parents' wishes but from whom he had been involuntarily separated. The other case involved Sándor Bródy (1863-1924), one of the most celebrated writers of his time. He was still an apprentice journalist in Kolozsvár when he was challenged by no less than six aristocrats for having published an article which they regarded as offensive.

Few if any clear signals forewarning the dramatic burst of Hungarian-Jewish fencers on the Olympic platform may be detected. Until 1908 Jewish fencers had not even gained national, let alone international, recognition. In fact, an air of some mystery surrounds the fencer who would become Hungary's first two-time Olympic saber champion in individual and team competition.

Dr. Jenő Fuchs (1882-1955) was decidedly unlike the dashing, graceful, slender, tall army officer whose image the public had customarily associated with the heroes of fencing. He was a quiet, unassuming man of slight build and small stature. He had belonged to no club, won no national championship, and placed only third in the qualifying competition on the basis of which the members of Hungary's Olympic fencing teams were selected. It is recalled, however, that in Budapest's best-known fencing clubs Fuchs had already been thought of as an indefatigably fierce, cool, and technically superb competitor. On London's open-air, gravel-surfaced piste Fuchs proved unstoppable. The finals looked more like those of a national rather than an Olympic championship. Of the eight finalists seven were Hungarians; the eighth, the lone "foreigner," was a Czech. Except for one foul—a technical penalty which both he and the Czech Goppold de Lobsdorf were assessed for failing to break a stalemate within the allotted time of eight minutes—Fuchs performed flawlessly. He overwhelmed his opponents. Yet even as he basked in the glitter of the Olympic gold he could hardly have remained indifferent to his unchallenged mastery of the best fencers of his country, whose championship he had never won.

The team competition revealed an equally if not more surprising spectacle of Hungarian-Jewish achievements. Four of the five members of the saber team Hungary fielded were Jews. They were, in addition to Fuchs, Dezső Földes (1880-1950), Oszkár Gerde (1883-1944), and Lajos Werkner (1883-1943). Interestingly, none had ever been a national champion prior to 1908. Földes would win a national épée title in 1910 and Werkner would become a three-time national saber champion in the years from 1912 to 1914. The Hungarians romped to the championship, defeating the Germans (who in the 1906 Hellenic Games had won the team title), the Italians, and, in the finals, the Czechs. The team from the "nation of fencers" triumphed on its first try; without its Jewish members the outcome might have been different.

In addition to the unique achievement of the Hungarian-Jewish fencers other notable performances wait to be salvaged from the statistical anonymity of record books. Two of the four members of Hungary's 200-meter freestyle relay swimming team who won silver medals were Jews. Like their more successful counterpart in fencing, neither had reached his full potential. Imre Zachár, a member of the *MTK* and a remarkably versatile swimmer, would win national championships in the 100-meter and the 800-meter freestyle and in river swimming (1910), and József Munk, also of the *MTK*, would win the 100-meter freestyle title in 1911. An unexpectedly cruel twist of fate prevented both from winning gold medals. Munk, Zachár, and Béla Las-Torres, the first three members of the team, swam in championship form, providing Zoltán Halmay, the anchor, a comfortable lead. He was nearly twelve meters ahead of Henry Taylor, his English counterpart. Halmay, the two-time Olympic gold medalist in the 50- and 100-meter freestyle in St. Louis, predictably increased the lead. As he approached the last 50-meter mark, tragedy struck. Halmay inexplicably lost strength, swam on the dividing rope and even hit his head on the wall of the pool. Thus instead of Hungary's red-white-green, which had already been placed at the base of the winners' flagpole, the Union Jack was raised.

In track and field, after twelve lean years, another Hungarian-Jewish athlete won an Olympic medal. Ödön Bodor-Krausz ran the last leg in the uneven distance relay (200, 200, 400, and 800 meters), giving Hungary the third-place finish behind the United States and Germany. He also placed fourth in the 800 meters. Hopes of an Olympic gold had been pinned on the performance of another Jewish athlete. In the spring of 1908 Mór Kovács-Kóczán, a would-be five-time national champion javelin thrower, broke the world record three times. His scores were 54.73, 57.02, and 57.08 meters. Either of the last two throws would have given him the Olympic gold (the eventual winner, the Swedish Erik Lemming, threw only 54.83 meters). However, in his first Olympic competition Kovács-Kóczán was woefully off-form and finished a disappointing fourth with a throw of 35 meters.

Similar expectations preceded the performance of Ödön Toldi. A talented swimmer in the 100- and 200-meter breaststroke, Toldi's career between 1906 and 1914 was highlighted by numerous national and international titles as well as Hungarian and world records. Unfortunately, he would reach the high-water mark of his development within three years after the 1908 Olympic Games. In 1910 and 1911 he swam world record times in 100- and 200-meter competitions. In London he placed fourth in the 200-meter breaststroke with 3:15.2, which was only 1.2 seconds slower than the time of the bronze medal winner, Sweden's Pontus Hanson.

The final tally shows that the achievements of Hungarian-Jewish Olympians at the fourth Olympic Games exceeded those of their predecessors both in number and diversity. The statistics, however, should give no cause for surprise. The 60-member Hungarian Olympic team was larger than all the previous teams combined, better organized and better financed. Moreover, the selection committee could draw from a far larger and rapidly growing number of Jewish athletes than in any previous periods of preparation for the Olympic Games.

In some crucial respects the 1912 Olympic Games in Stockholm witnessed a remarkably self-confident repeat performance by Hungarian-Jewish Olympians. It emerged out of an atmosphere of ambitious and optimistic expectations. In the course of correspondence between Coubertin and Ferenc Kemény, the idea of holding the 1916 Olympic Games in Budapest had been launched, leading to a meeting of the International Olympic Committee in the Hungarian capital in May 1911. No less inspiring was the government's approval of an Olympic budget of 58,000 crowns, which allowed the Hungarian Olympic Committee to select a 130-member team. In addition, a sudden outburst of interest in the

Olympic Games in Hungarian newspapers whetted the public's appetite. The whole country seemed to rally around the Olympic team in a spirit of frenzied unity, unprecedented in the brief history of Hungary's Olympic involvement. Ultimately winning twenty-nine medals, the team was to prove no cause for disappointment.

Again the Hungarian hero of the Olympic Games was Dr. Jenő Fuchs; again the Hungarians dominated the saber competition, both in the individual and the team events. Four of the twelve-member Olympic team— Fuchs, Dezső Földes, Oszkár Gerde, and Lajos Werkner—were Jews. One hundred and twenty-eight Olympians, divided into sixteen groups, clashed for the privilege of representing their countries in the ultimate round robin. As had happened four years earlier, seven Hungarians and one "foreigner" —the Italian Nedo Nadi, who won the Olympic gold in the individual épée competition—reached the finals. Fuchs and two army officers, Ervin Mészáros and Béla Békessy, were regarded as having the best chance of sharing the medals. Only the sequence was in doubt. Mészáros beat Békessy and Fuchs suffered an unexpected, painful defeat at the hands of another Hungarian finalist, Zoltán Schenker, who eventually placed sixth. At that point Mészáros looked like a sure winner. However, he was subsequently defeated by Péter Tóth, a clubmate, and by Fuchs, leaving Békessy and Fuchs to decide the outcome of the finals. It was a classic clash of contrasting styles. The short, unimpressive-looking Fuchs, a patient but lightning-quick defensive artist, proved to be the master of the tall, slender, quintessentially dashing Békessy. One last quick victory over the Italian Nadi, and the jubilant Fuchs could again rest on Olympic laurels.

The team competition was much the same. The Hungarians were so strong that any combination of four was believed to be a shoo-in. As in London, Jewish fencers were predictably dominant. Four of the eight-member Hungarian saber team were Jews. In a field of twelve, the Hungarians advanced firmly to the finals, where they defeated the Austrians 11-5 and the Dutch 13-3. The lion's share of victory was again Fuch's. Of sixteen bouts he lost only one.

The winner of four Olympic gold medals was one of the most enigmatic figures in the history of Hungarian fencing. A cool, meticulously calculating competitor who in the Olympian heights baffled the often reckless practitioners of the offensive style with an artful display of defensive moves, Fuchs was a different man in the more mundane walks of life. He was argumentative, oversensitive, and given to frequent outbursts of anger. He was disdainful of authority and would join no club. He managed to alienate most of Hungary's top fencers and the officials of the Hungarian Athletic Federation. Fuchs deviated from his singularly nonconformist ways only once. After he won his first two Olympic gold medals in London, he accepted Brüll's invitation to head the newly established (October 1908) fencing department of the *MTK*. Under Fuch's leadership the young *MTK* team, consisting of only Jewish fencers (Róbert Sacher, Tivadar Weisz, József Beck, and Henrik Fodor) finished a respectable fifth in the national championship. However, not even a friendly and respectful environment could change the recalcitrant Fuchs. He left the *MTK* within a year and a half, early in 1910. For nearly two years he did not compete. He took up rowing, competing—predictably—only in the singles. He emerged from his self-imposed exile in time to astonish the members of the selection committee for the 1912 Olympic Games with his remarkable technique. Having won two more Olympic medals, Fuchs again disappeared—for twelve years. In 1924 he resurfaced to participate in the Olympic trials but inexplicably lost heart after learning that the International Fencing Federation had reduced to four the number of participants a country was permitted to name to the individual competition. Four years later he tried again. In the qualifying rounds he drew Ervin Mészáros, his Olympic teammate in 1912, who was also attempting a comeback. The two aging eminences, the story goes, faced each other in front of a large group of hushed spectators. Both defensive specialists, the bout was expected to be one filled with carefully planned, albeit time-consuming, meticulously executed maneuvers. It never got under way. After a few minutes of virtual inaction, Mészáros pulled off his helmet. "Dear Jenő," he asked, "don't you think this isn't for us anymore?" Fuchs nodded. "Let's call it quits, then." Quietly and for once in agreement, Fuchs ended his competitive career, one of the most illustrious in the annals of Hungarian fencing.

Few Hungarian officials had nurtured hopes of a medal-winning performance by the gymnastics team. No Hungarian had won a medal or even placed in any of the previous Olympic Games. Much to everyone's surprise, the Hungarian team captured second place behind the Italian. Three Jewish gymnasts were among the recipients of the coveted silver medals: Imre Gellért, Samu Fóti, and Jenő Tittich.

Hungary's sole medal in track and field was won by a Jewish athlete. Undeterred by his heartrending performance in London, Mór Kovács-Kóczán's unflagging determination, boundless willpower, and unquenchable thirst for success strengthened his position as Hungary's preeminent javelin thrower. He continued to train hard and competed with stubborn determination. He won two national championships in 1911 and 1912, thereby earning the nod from the selection committee for the 1912 Olympic Games. In Stockholm he lived up to expectations; with a throw of 55.50 meters he won the bronze medal. The Olympic success gave a boost to his career. He won three more national titles in 1913-14 and 1918. This dependable and durable athlete may have had a good chance to win another medal either in 1916 or 1920. His winning throw in the 1914 national championship was more than two meters longer than his Olympic best.

In Stockholm and long after the 1912 Olympic Games critical remarks were often made about Swedish judges. They, it was alleged, consistently voted against or reduced the scores of anyone whom they regarded as a threat to the chances of Swedish Olympians to win medals. The Jewish Ödön Radvány is said to have been victimized by unfair scoring. A talented lightweight, as a youngster he was advised against wrestling because of his fragile constitution, but by doing gymnastic exercises and using various pieces of body-building equipment, he developed a powerfully muscular body. Radvány combined raw strength with a virtually inexhaustible reservoir of technical maneuvers. Between 1909 and 1922 he had no equal in Hungary as a competitor, and later as a coach he trained generations of wrestlers with his revolutionary methods. The "School of Radvány" soon became an internationally respected and imitated training method and a blueprint for competition. Though he had made no mark in the books of Olympic statistics in 1908, Radvány had become one of the preeminent lighweight wrestlers by the time he was selected to be an Olympian in 1912. He had won the first of his nine Hungarian championships in 1909 and a European title in 1912. Thus he was given more than an outside chance to win an Olympic medal. Like Kovács-Kóczán, he regarded his failure to do so as an unfortunate incident. He again won the European title in 1913 and became world champion in 1920 and 1922. The real culprits that frustrated Radvány's Olympic hopes were politics and time. The outbreak of World War I and Hungary's immediate postwar loss of respect in the international community caused the Hungarian Olympians to go into a twelve-year-long eclipse.

Few emotions soar higher and are treasured more than the ones that accompany the unfolding spectacle of Olympic competition. Indeed, for hundreds of millions of people around the world the Olympic Games provide an opportunity once every four years to watch the best in athletic competition and savor moments of nationalistic pride. For constancy, accessibility, frequency, and familiarity, however, the Olympic Games do not measure up to the events that take place on the national level. Nothing is dearer to the heart of a true-blue fan than to root for his favorite athlete or team and to passionately boo those who in his eyes can do nothing right. Thus whereas the Olympic fever overtakes him only once every four years, there is scarcely a weekend when he may not shout for joy at a local victory or breathe fire as the occasion dictates. Furthermore, participation in Olympic competition is not the final verdict on ability and potential. Financial restrictions and political pressures were two of the most easily discernible impediments to the Hungarians' quest to reach their full potential in the five Olympic Games before World War I. Personal circumstances irreconcilable with the demands of the arduous Olympic preparations, untimely injuries, simply being off-form, or adverse decisions of judges devastate many an Olympic hopeful during the all-important tryouts. Limitations imposed by the International Olympic Committee on the number of participants in events often thwarted the plans of selection committees to field the best team possible and shattered the Olympic dreams of some of Hungary's best athletes.

In addition to the Olympic medal winners, there were athletes who only placed in Olympic competition, rarely managing to escape relegation to statistical oblivion, others who did not don the Olympic uniform even once in their careers, yet were selected to represent Hungary in international competition, and still others who never experienced the exhilaration of sharing in the ultimate recognition of ability—and often proof of popularity—as members of national or Olympic teams. All of them found their way into the good graces of loyal and bighearted fans and the make-believe world of star-struck and imaginative children, who imitated them and even pretended to be them.

From the dawn of organized sports in Hungary in the last quarter of the nineteenth century to the outbreak of the First World War Jewish athletes were as visible in national competition as they were in the Olympic Games. Except for the stubbornly independent Fuchs, whom any club would have

dearly loved to count as its member but who successfully defied the con-
fining atmosphere of organizations to the end of his phenomenal career
as a competitive fencer, Jewish athletes represented a variety of clubs,
both in Budapest and the provinces, in national competition. Their chances
to develop club affiliations were promising, though predictably slow in
coming. Along with the positive outlook of pedagogues on physical education, which undoubtedly served as the earliest means of introduction to
sports for many a future Jewish champion, sport clubs proved to be the
true vehicles of athletic success. By 1870 there were thirteen functioning
sport clubs in Hungary.

The glamor boys of sporting life were adventurous aristocrats who defied the rigid social code of their class, and dashing army officers, fired
more by the love of betting—and danger and dueling—than the love of
sport. Few if any Jewish athletes could hope to join the most highly developed sport club, founded by Count Miksa Eszterházy upon his return
from a tour of England in 1875. The Magyar Atlétikai Club, or *MAC*, was
modeled on London's Amateur Athletic Club. It ushered in a new, fast-
paced era in the development of organized sport in Hungary. Though its
principal founders and supporters were liberal nationalists, the *MAC* was
a bastion of Hungary's exclusivist upper crust. Jewish athletes had to wait
more than a decade before the proponents of various branches of athletics
and the advocates of gymnastic virtues began to found clubs in the late
1870s.

No documentary evidence suggests that in the dawn of organized sports
in Hungary Jewish athletes were forced to join certain clubs due to a lack
of alternatives. Except for the *MAC*, they could be found representing a
variety of clubs, such as the Nemzeti (Pesti) Torna Egylet (*NTE*, "National Gymnastics Association of Pest," est. 1866), the Újpesti Torna Egylet
(*UTE*, "Gymnastics Association of Újpest," est. 1885), the Budapest III. ker.
Torna és Vívó Egylet (III ker. *TVE*, "Gymnastics and Fencing Association
of Budapest's Third District," est. 1887), and the Ferencvárosi Torna
Club (*FTC*, "Gymnastics Club of Ferencváros," est. 1899).

There was one club, the *MTK*, whose very initials became identified
with Hungary's Jewry in the eyes of Jews and non-Jews alike. However,
the *MTK* was never an exclusively Jewish sport club, though perhaps it
had more Jewish members than all other clubs combined. It was founded
in the aftermath of an athletic competition held on 10 September 1888

on the sprawling grounds of a villa owned by the Freudigers, a family of wealthy Jewish industrialists. Most of the day's participants were members of the Nemzeti (Pesti) Torna Egylet and all happened to be Jewish. When the leaders of the gymnastics-oriented *NTE* admonished club members for participating in an athletic competition, the latter defied their leadership and decided to form a new club. Although some of its founders and many members, perhaps gradually the majority, were non-Jews, the *MTK* turned out to be a haven for Jewish sportsmen and an enduring monument to their achievements.

Except for horsemanship and rowing, traditionally dominated by aristocrats, Jewish sportsmen, both as organizers and competitors, were present at the birth of virtually every sport in Hungary. In the initial stage of development, from the latter half of the nineteenth century to the outbreak of the First World War, their achievements attest to a convincing display of determination and versatility, physical prowess and skill, endurance and competitiveness.

No generation of administrators faced challenges as great as the ones who laid the groundwork of organized sport. They had no predecessors and thus had to create precedents and gain experience by trial and error. Hindered by the scarcity of funds, facilities and equipment, they sought out patrons. In the constant search for talent they had to overcome obstacles such as suspicious parents and timid youngsters from whom physical education and sport were mysterious, uncharted waters. Failures were few and of short duration. At the end they were allowed to savor the taste of success. The growing popularity of sports and the ever-improving achievements of the competitors were the fruits of their unending efforts.

As progress in any form in the latter half of the nineteenth century originated in middle-class initiative, the presence of Jews among the earliest organizers and administrators of sport in Hungary seemed a foregone conclusion. Ferenc Kemény was Hungary's contribution to the small group that nurtured the renascent spirit of the Olympic Games and the driving force behind the Hungarian Olympic Committee. Alfréd Brüll, the other pioneer Olympic activist, was the quintessential club leader who was to be the informing spirit of the *MTK* for four decades before the outbreak of the Second World War. They left not only the legacy of wisdom, foresight, and athletic excellence that was to become an unwritten code of conduct for all future generations of Hungarian sports leaders, but also a sobering reminder of pitfalls that could trip and fell even the idols of sport. Kemény, a dreamer-turned-realist who helped conquer the past, fell victim to the petty sentiments of envy, jealousy and narrow-mindedness that touched off a fratricidal strife involving the members of the National Olympic Committee and meddlesome outsiders. Brüll, a man of sweeping vision yet a firm realist who brought a unique manager-ial style to the practice of sport leadership, perished in the brutal finale of the rule of the fanatically anti-Semitic Arrow Cross government of Ferenc Szálasi.

Following closely in the footsteps of Kemény and Brüll, Jewish activists, organizers, and coaches made invaluable contributions to sports in Hun-gary in the decades before the First World War. In swimming, the first sport to provide a Jewish athlete, Alfréd Hajós-Guttmann, the means to Olympic immortality, Ödön Boros, György Donáth, Pál Hay, and Alfréd Schibert were among the first generation of organizers. Boros was execu-tive secretary of the Hungarian Swimming Federation and Schibert its secretary. Donáth acquired international reputation as executive secretary of the European Swimming League. He was instrumental in the develop-ment of organized swimming in Szeged, then Hungary's second largest city. Two Jewish members of the *MTK*, an early powerhouse in com-petitive swimming in Hungary, were also among the founding fathers of the Hungarian Swimming Federation after they had spearheaded a drive for organizational independence from the Hungarian Athletic Federation, to which swimming had belonged. Henrik Vida, a former diver, and Gyula Dezsényi-Deutsch, one of the best Hungarian swimmers before the turn of the century, helped the Federation take its first uncertain steps. It came as a surprise to no one that Brüll should become the president of the Federation in 1906. In athletics, Lajos Vermes, the first president of the *MTK*, the club with the longest participation in that sport, was a pioneer organizer. He was also instrumental in introducing the velocipede and supervised its growth into competitive cycling.

Few events in the development of wrestling in Hungary took place without the participation of Brüll, who started his multidimensional role in Hungarian sports as the president of the wrestling section of the Hun-garian Athletic Federation and later became a nationally and internation-ally recognized leader in the Hungarian Wrestling Federation and the

International Wrestling Federation. Following his victory at the 1908 Olympic Games, Richárd Weisz, Hungary's most famous prewar wrestling champion, became a coach of the *MTK*. Drawing on his immensely successful competitive career in that sport, he was idolized and imitated by generations of young wrestlers.

One of the most effective protagonists of wrestling in Hungary was Jenő Radvány, an erstwhile gymnast whose brother Ödön was one of the luminaries of the post-Weisz era of Jewish champions. Like Brüll, he was an industrialist and would acquire a reputation as a tireless official of both the national and international federations of wrestling.

Predictably, the activities of Jews in the noncompetitive areas of fencing compared favorably with the performance and achievement of Jewish fencers. The standard set by the latter, to be sure, was uncommonly high. In light of the four Olympic gold medals won by Jenő Fuchs, all other efforts may look somewhat dim. Still, there were some notable contributions by Jewish supporters of organized fencing. Marcel Hajdu (1871-1936), a lawyer, a politician, and a fencer of not inconsiderable skill, was the founder and president of the prestigious Nemzeti Vívó Club ("National Fencing Club") and the noncompeting leader of the Hungarian Olympic saber team that won gold medals in 1912. He was also the president of the fencing section of the Hungarian Athletic Federation and later the executive vice-president of the newly founded Hungarian Fencing Federation. Other Jewish functionaries were Móric Domony, Lajos Werkner (a three-time national saber champion and a member of the gold-medal-winning Olympic teams in 1908 and 1912), Tibor Schwartz, József Fodor, Jenő Pick, József Beck, Artúr Lehner, and Gyula Sótér. However, only four nationally famous Jewish fencing masters, Károly Fodor, Ármin Róna, Benő Bach, and Alfréd Gellér, may actually be cited. An even more puzzling phenomenon was the inability of the leaders of the *MTK* to start one outstanding fencer in national competition, let alone field a first-rate fencing team. Most Jewish members of the *MTK*'s fencing department were gentlemanly dilettants who preferred the glitter and pagentry of year-end exhibitions to the rigorous demands of regular competition. However, in 1908 Brüll personally undertook the task of carrying out a sweeping overhaul of the department. He and ninety-three other members signed up a fencers. Brüll even persuaded the irascible Fuchs to join as coach. Soon *MTK* fencers started participating in tournaments, but without notable success. Within two years the *MTK* and

Fuchs, to no one's surprise, parted ways. He was followed by the Jewish
fencing masters Aladár Radó and Henrik Fodor. Neither could work
miracles. The leaders of the *MTK* used untested methods in the hope of
inducing fast-paced development and gaining quick results in a sport that
was difficult and time-consuming to learn and for which the odds of
failure were great. Their plan backfired. The club that would provide a
platform to Jewish athletes in their quest for national and international
fame in a variety of sports failed in fencing, a sport in which Jewish members representing other clubs became members of Hungary's national
team. The national team in turn became for decades the virtually invincible force in international and Olympic competition.

In comparison with the high visibility of Jewish functionaries in other
sports, gymnastics proved frustratingly uninviting. The Magyar Atlétikai
Club, Hungary's largest and most prestigious place of sportsminded men,
accepted no Jews as members; whereas the leaders of Nemzeti Torna
Egylet proved excessively zealous in reproaching those of its Jewish members who participated in unauthorized athletic competition. Small wonder
that no documentary evidence suggests that Jewish officials had an active
role in the establishment (1885) and running of the Magyarországi Torna
Egyletek Országos Szövetsége (*MOTESZ*, "National Federation of Hungarian Gymnastics Associations"), even though many young Jewish men
enthusiastically supported and participated in gymnastics competition
and some of Hungary's earliest champions were Jews. Again the *MTK*
would become the catalyst in the production of Jewish gymnastics officials. Henrik Vida, its executive secretary, was named head of the national
gymnastics team that represented Hungary in the 1908 Olympic Games,
and Manó Vágó worked tirelessly to help the *MTK* discharge its principal
duty in gymnastics, the development of physical education among the
masses.

Jews participated in and made significant contributions to the development of physical education among the increasingly numerous industrial
workers, a segment of the population about which the planners of the
prewar capitalist system and guardians of its class distinctions felt that
the less that was known the better. The interests of both groups were
threatened, but in addition the Jewish leaders of the establishment were
embarrassed by the growing number of their coreligionists who took an
active role in the workers' movement. Its implications were lost on few,

especially the political anti-Semites, who wasted little time in spreading the warning of the "Judeo-Bolshevik menace." They were not hampered by the lack of names and examples in substantiating their allegations. A. Karr and M. Mittelmann were elected into the executive committee of the newly founded (1870) General Workers' Association; Zsigmond Politzer was named editor of the *Arany Trombita* ("Gold Clarion"), the official organ of the movement; Jakab Kürschner was instrumental in the organization of the Workers' Insurance Fund; Leó Frankel had a leading role in the establishment of the Socialist Party and subsequently was one of the most highly visible participants in the Paris Commune of 1871; Samu Jászai guided the development of the trade union movement and was elected to high positions in both its national and internatinal organizations and into the Hungarian Parliament, where he represented Social Democratic views; and Vilmos Mezőfi was a leading organizer of the agricultural laborers' movement. The Jewish origin of many founding members of trade unions was also easily discernible. Thus the list of Jews affected by the persecution and trials of prominent Socialists was predictably long, giving the critics of the emancipation and assimilation of Hungarian Jewry a virtually inexhaustible reservoir of ammunition for demagogic attacks. Interestingly, the year 1896 turned out to be one in which a puzzling variety of conflicting events converged, causing no negligible problems in the long run for Hungary's Jews. For them the sweet taste of their manifold contributions to the success of the millennial celebrations and remarkable achievements in the first Olympic Games of modern times would be soured by the large and noisy demonstrations of workers on May 1. The police dispersed the crowd by a brutal show of force, reinforcing the notion of the "Judeo-Bolshevik menace" by putting many of the Jewish leaders under surveillance or house arrest. No less embarrassing for them was the publication of the Hungarian-born Theodor Herzl's *Der Judenstaat,* the bible of political Zionism, which formulated a Jewish nationalist philosophy that clashed with the pronounced Magyar nationalism of Hungary's Neolog Jews.

Long before the decision was reached at the Second International (London 1896) concerning the utility of the workers' physical exercise associations in the struggle for the overthrow of the capitalist social order and development of the ideal socialist state, plans facilitating the participation of the workers in chess, mountain climbing, hiking, bicycling, and gymnastics were adopted into the program of the short-lived Budapest Workers' Association (1868). A more productive and influential organization, however, was not formed until after the turn of the century. In 1905 the Workers' Gymnastics Association (Munkás Testedző Egylet, or *MTE*) came into being. Of its three-member presidential council two, Fülöp Grünhut and Dezső Bíró, were Jewish. Bíró was also the principal organizer of the Workers' Sport Federation.

Not all organizations that catered to the workers' burgeoning love of sport were established by sport-minded socialist activists or were inextricably interwoven with the political philosophy of the socialist movement. Similar initiatives were often made by those of privileged status at the other extreme of the social spectrum. Sport-loving industrialists invested considerable sums, time and effort in forming factory-based sport clubs. In Csepel and Újpest, two predominantly working-class suburbs of Budapest, interesting—and rare—examples of interclass cooperation may be cited, involving the activities of two prominent Jewish financiers, Lipót Aschner (1872-1952) founded and became president of the Újpesti Torna Egylet (*UTE,* "Gymnastics Association of Újpest"), one of Hungary's most famous sport clubs. He was a generous contributor to all worthy sport projects. Baron Manfréd Weiss (1857-1922), whose factory in Csepel was the first in Hungary to manufacture munitions, provided the means for the establishment of the Csepel Sport Club.

The participation of the "untouchables" of Hungary's capitialist and class-conscious society in sports, as fans or as participants, ensured the success of what in the long run would become the most popular of them all. In its simplest and purest form the ingredients of soccer consist of a patch of land, four piles of clothes to create the illusion of goalposts, and two teams of equal size, kicking a mostly round object made of small pieces of cloth twisted around or sewn together. Small wonder that discriminating gentlemen, for whom certain sports were pastimes of questionable taste and limited to the socially underprivileged, objected to the sounds and sights of soccer. Their sensibilities, accustomed to the refined, graceful, quiet elegance that tennis and riding imparted, were offended by a bunch of sweaty and noisy men running up and down on an ill-defined field, chasing an oddly shaped ball and often colliding with reckless abandon, causing pain and injury. Soccer was a "sport for wild men," concluded some members of Parliament, and only the customary snail's pace of the parliamentary proceedings prevented them from adopting a proposal to ban it. However, soccer caught on and became Hungary's most popular sport.

Even though the grass roots of soccer in Hungary neither attracted nor involved Jewish participation—the most deprived segments of the population had been especially vulnerable to religious traditions and the new political exponents of anti-Semitism—much of its success and popularity may be attributed to the work of Jewish organizers. The Magyar Labdarúgó Szövetség (*MLSZ*, "Hungarian Soccer Federation," est. 1901) greatly benefited from the activities of the indefatigable Alfréd Büll, Samu Kaffka, Dezső Vadász, Henrik Fodor, Hugó Steiner, and Henrik Vida. Lajos Tibor was elected copresident of the federation. His principal aides, Lajos Taubner and Gyula Baján, Tivadar Kiss and Emil Neuwelt, modernized the structure of the federation and put it on a stable financial foundation. Ottó Reichardt was instrumental in enlisting the support of university students and Dezső Bíró organized a network of soccer clubs among the workers. Perhaps the first internationally known Hungarian soccer leader was Mór Fischer. A mechanical engineer by profession, Fischer spent some time in England studying the railroad system, especially its welfare institutions. He recognized the social benefits of sport and on his return to Hungary became president of the Törekvés Sport Club. His social views led him to establish the Railroad Workers' Sport Federation. Because of his growing reputation abroad and familiarity with foreign languages and institutions, Fischer was selected to represent the Hungarian Soccer Federation in the preparation of international matches and its international relations. The highlight of Fischer's career came in 1927 when he was elected president of the International Soccer Federation (*FIFA*).

In the era of uncertain beginnings before the First World War, the preparation of the national team for international matches was a nightmare for coaches and members of the selection committee alike. Yet they gradually succeeded in transforming a confused, purposeless group of players, for whom the ball was merely an object to kick as far as possible, into a national eleven playing soccer with dedication, concentration, steadily improving technique, and almost methodical teamwork. The performance of the Hungarian team in the prewar decade left lingering bittersweet memories, ranging from seesaw results againt Austria and virtually predestined defeats by England to winning the consolation round final against Austria in the 1912 Olympic Games in Stockholm. To the difficult task of guiding this national team from public embarrassment to international recognition, Jewish officials, the likes of Ede Hercog and Gyula Kiss, who is said to have been the greatest authority on soccer of his time, made important contributions.

Introduced in the 1870s and principally utilized as a means of transportation, the velocipede quickly captured the hearts of Hungarians and whetted the appetite of those who looked beyond the apparent limitations of the strange-looking contraption. The bond of speed between rider and machine became a natural test of prowess, determination, endurance, and skill. Few sports in Hungary attracted such immediate and devout following among Jews as cycling. Sándor Hegedüs, a dentist by profession, was instrumental in organizing the Budapest Cycling Club at the end of the 1890s. His counterparts in the provinces were Hermann A. Schwartz, one of the earliest champions, and Simon Hauser, who laid the foundation of cycling clubs for those to whom Budapest was out of reach. Other Jewish officials who made vital contributions to the early history of cycling in Hungary were Béla Halász and Ármin Eichner. The largest and most successful cycling organization was that of the *MTK*—as early as 1890 it could boast of twenty-three registered cyclists—the fruit of the labors of such outstanding Jewish organizers of the sport as Ferenc Fodor, Hugó Steiner (the executive secretary of the club), and Dezső Wachsmann.

The activities of Jewish officials and the achievements of Jewish athletes helped to advance the cause of sport and physical education on the national scene. They also helped Hungary to establish a reputation of excellence in European, world, and Olympic competition, thereby delighting the liberal politicians who had supported the emancipation of the Jews, the leaders of the Neologs, for whom Magyarization, patriotism, and reform of religious and communal tradition were the only practicable means of reaching the same goals. Yet when in 1906 a sport club was formed in Budapest the applause suddenly stopped. Few people detected the reason. It was a small club with limited potentials, providing facilities for only three sports, fencing, athletics, and gymnastics. Its name, Vívó és Atlétikai Club (*VAC*, "Fencing and Athletic Club"), was inocuous enough. The founder of the *VAC* was Lajos Dömény, a twenty-six-year-old lawyer. So far so good. However, nothing below the façade conformed to the prevailing self-image and philosophy of Hungarian Jewry. Dömény was a devout Zionist, the founder of the Hungarian branch of the Keren Kayemet le-Yisrael, the Jewish National Fund of the World Zionist Organization, set up in 1901 to purchase and develop land in Palestine for future Zionist settlements. He also founded the Kadimah, an organization of Jewish boy scouts and, with Ármin Bokor, the *Zsidó Néplap* (Jewish People's Journal), the first Zionist publication in Hungary.

The assimilationist National Bureau of Magyar Israelites, which treated Zionism and its principal leaders, Theodor Herzl and Max Nordau, both Hungarian-born, with unabating hostility, was no more well-disposed toward Dömény and the *VAC,* which became Hungary's solely Jewish sport club. The *VAC* was anathema on two counts. Jewish athletes were rarely if ever identified by their religion and were expected to compete in the colors of whichever club they chose without regard for such considerations. The exclusive Jewish membership of Dömény's *VAC* defied that unwritten law. Furthermore, it had come into being in response to Nordau's "muscular Judaism," the theme he developed in a speech before the Fifth Zionist Congress in 1901, calling for the renewal of Jewish interest in sport and physical education, rather than as a consequence of the appeal of the Hungarian Jewish leadership to the same end.

Despite the atmosphere of suspicion that surrounded it, the *VAC* was not an entirely unwelcome phenomenon on the sport scene. Apparently there were enough Jewish athletes who were either sympathetic to Zionism, or disagreed with the philosophy of the assimilation-centered Jewish leadership, or were apprehensive about the remaining vestiges of anti-Semitism. They gave the *VAC* the stamp of approval. To them it became a haven, nurturing strong bonds of social and athletic camaraderie. Interestingly, the forty-year-long history of the *VAC,* highly successful in competitive achievement, has failed to attract the attention of the minuscule group of researchers and writers on the contributions of Jews in sport. They identify only Hakoach of Vienna, Bar Kochba of Berlin, and Hagibor of Prague.

The *VAC* had earned the right to be added to this short list. Except for the first few relatively undistinguished years of its existence, the *VAC* was far more than just another sport club. In 1913 the two best gymnasts of the *MTK* transferred to the *VAC.* Imre Gellért, a silver medal winner in team gymnastics in the 1912 Olympic Games and a three-time all-round national champion (1909, 1911, and 1912), and József Szalai, a would-be (1926) winner of the national all-round title, provided the *VAC* national recognition, which it subsequently solidified when many of its members were tapped for the national teams.

Despite the paucity of reliable statistical data and the scarcity of primary sources about the earliest appearance of Jewish athletes in national competition, it is safe to assume that the two most easily discernible traits of late-nineteenth-century Jewish life in Hungary—the official attitude of the government and the assimilationist philosophy of the Jewish leadership—had created an inviting atmosphere and an accommodating environment. Still, at the dawn of competitive sports and sport clubs, the Jewish men who chose to take full advantage of the prevailing conditions were breaking new ground, succeeding in one of the least cultivated areas of Jewish experience.

Unhappily the search for clues to help set the stage for the entry of Hungarian-Jewish athletes in competitive sports yields no tangible results. How did the earliest Jewish athletes become interested in areas of activity in which their forebears had not participated? What was the reaction of relatives and friends to a decision to participate in an activity that must surely have been regarded as un-Jewish? What kind of reception were Jewish athletes accorded when they first appeared at training sessions and in competition? No information has come to light that would help the researcher to find even partial answers to such questions.

The earliest references available shed light only on already well-known Jewish athletes and their achievements. From the outset there was no shortage in either, and as time went on both increased in number, quality, and diversity. The first sport that catapulted a Hungarian Jew into fame was swimming. Alfréd Hajós-Guttmann, the double gold medal winner at the 1896 Olympic Games in Athens, has cast a long shadow over the sport. However, he was by no means Hungarian Jewry's sole claim to swimming fame. In the 1890s the dominant Hungarian long-distance swimmer and one of Europe's best, Gyula Dezsényi-Deutsch, captured a number of national titles and won against Europe's best in the so-called Austrian Derby—a medley consisting of 1088, 510- and 68-meter events—and the Vienna championship. It is interesting to note that the available statistical data suggest that Hajós-Guttmann's younger brother, Henrik, had the longer and more varied swimming career of the two. Between 1905 and

1911 he won twenty national freestyle championships on long distance (880 yards and 1 mile) as well as in the extraordinarily demanding river-swimming event. Ödön Toldi, Henrik Hajós-Guttmann's contemporary, was a three-time national champion (in 1909, 1910, and 1911) in the 200-meter breaststroke and won in a number of international meets. The decade just before the First World War proved unusually auspicious for other Jewish swimmers as well. In 1907 and 1911 Imre Zachár won national titles in the 100-yard and 880-yard freestyle respectively. József Munk swam to victory in the 100-yard freestyle national championship in 1911 and László Szentgróth in 1913. Breaststrokers Imre Elek and Andor Bakonyi set world records, and other top-flight swimmers were Leó Donáth, Kornél Hendl, and Pál Hay.

Water polo became another almost natural expression of the Jews' interest in sports. Three Jewish players were named to Hungary's first Olympic team (1912), which placed an undistinguished sixth, giving no clues to future greatness. Tibor Fazekas was one of the best Hungarian players in his twenty-two-year-long (1910-32) career. Between 1912 and 1928 he was a member of Hungary's national team thirty-two times. He played for the *FTC,* a team that between 1910 and 1927 won twelve national championships. According to some chroniclers of that sport, Fazekas was one of the earliest Hungarian world-class water polo players. Even though he could not match Fazekas in career statistics, Sándor Ádám had impressive qualifications on the basis of which he was selected to play on the Olympic squad. He was a member of the Magyar Úszó Egylet (*MUE*), helping it win national championships from 1906 to 1909, and subsequently he played for the *FTC,* when it won three consecutive (1911-13) national titles. In 1912-13 Ádám played three times on the national team of Hungary. The third Jewish player was Imre Zachár, the sole representative of the *MTK.* A versatile swimmer who was as much at home in short distances that demanded explosive speed as in long distances requiring endurance and consistency, Zachár won national championships in both the 100-yard and 800-yard freestyle. He played twice on the national water polo team in 1912. He was one of the few players who made the difficult transition from swimming to water polo with great success.

It was in 1912, the year of the Stockholm Olympic Games, that a young man joined the *MTK* in search of fame as a sidestroker. It was an ill-conceived idea. The style was destined to quick expiration and the young man's physical attributes held out no promise for an outstanding career in swimming. He then switched to water polo, and this time fortune smiled on him. Béla Komjádi quickly learned the intricacies of the game and became a player of whom it was said that his speed and swimming did not measure up to his technical skill and unabating determination. A crippling wound in the First World War would end his career as a player but left his love of water polo undiminished. He would soon emerge as the principal architect of Hungary's "golden team" of the interwar years. His name is uttered with reverence and his contributions are vividly remembered, decades after his premature death in 1933.

Scant statistical data and indistinct references hinder the work of identifying the outstanding Jewish athletes who made contributions to the development of track and field events in Hungary. Still some names, forming an undoubtedly incomplete list, have emerged to provide a representative sampling. Jewish athletes consistently appeared in national and international meets since their inception, and acquitted themselves creditably. In addition to Gyula Kellner and Dezső Wein, the two 1896 Olympians, a growing number of Jewish runners joined the elite circle of champions. In the middle distances, Gyula Malcsiner won six national titles and Béla Brandl proved a steady, reliable competitor. Ármin Weisz, a sprinter, became a five-time national champion, and József Szenes captured the 100-meter national title in 1915. Hugó Rosenthal, Miksa Váradi-Weiszhausz, and Róbert Abarbanell ranked among Hungary's best long-distance runners. Other well-known runners of the period include Emil Déri, Ármin Horner, Jenő Rákos, Pál Szalay, and József and György Weinreb. Béla Helfer was a champion hurdler. In long-distance walking Jewish athletes established a virtual monopoly. Arnold Kohn won his first national championship in 1889. His title was subsequently claimed and held by Miksa Grünwald and Jenő Vidor.

The participation and achievement of Jewish competitors in field events were equally impressive. Long jumpers Lajos Tótisz, Ödön Holics, and Andor Szende alternated in winning national championships and numerous other titles. In 1915 Dezső Farkas became the national shot put champion. Jewish champions also left their mark on two events of brief duration and ephemeral fame. Lipót Sachs won championships in the high long jump, and Sándor Freund in the vertical shot put.

Jewish participation in wrestling—exclusively in the Greco-Roman style —was inevitable. The best of them all was Richárd Weisz, the 1908 heavyweight Olympic champion, who after prematurely retiring from competition spent the rest of his life coaching. A less compelling presence was that of the lightweight Ödön Radvány. Though as an Olympian he was not Weisz's equal, he was peerless among the innovators and theoreticians of wrestling in Hungary. In addition to these two internationally known Jewish champions, others left their mark in the record books. Miklós Grosz was the lightweight national champion in 1908, the year before Radvány won the first of his five national titles in the same weight class. Weisz had a worthy successor in both categories in which he won national championships. In the middleweight, József Előd captured the national title in 1908 and retained it for two consecutive years. Then he moved up to the heavyweight division that was the exclusive monopoly of the Jewish wrestlers of the *MTK*.

Between 1904 and 1909 Weisz reigned, challenged but unbeaten. Only slightly less impressive—except for the Olympic comparison—was Tibor Fischer's record of achievements. He proved a worthy successor to Weisz, winning the national title four times (1910-12 and 1914). He was a durable competitor, winning his fifth national championship in 1920. Repeating Weisz's successful move from the ranks of the middleweights to those of the heavyweights, Előd deposed Fischer in 1913 for his only title in that division. The achievements of these three Jewish wrestlers marked one of the most remarkable epochs in Hungarian sports. From 1904 to 1920, except for a four-year period that included the First World War and a 1918 victory by a non-Jewish wrestler, Weisz, Fischer, and Előd ruled the heavyweight division.

Just as the wrestlers presented Hungarian Jewry with a new well-muscled image of itself, so did the Hungarian-Jewish gymnasts. Dávid Müller was the *MTK*'s gymnast, the best in Hungary from 1888 to 1896 and regarded as the most beautifully proportioned Hungarian. Other well-known Jewish gymnasts were Emil Kosinger, Endre Gutwillig, Henrik Fodor and Pál Müller. The first Jewish gymnast who entered the record books was Imre Gellért, also of the *MTK*. He was a two-time Olympian (1908 and 1912) and a three-time all-round national champion (1909, 1911-12). A gifted painter by profession, Gellért is remembered as a gymnast who could transform even the simplest movements into artistic and dynamically flowing exercises. He died in Los Angeles in 1981 at the age of ninety-one.

In fencing Jenő Fuchs's unpredictable and erratic personality gave the national championships and other competitions an almost perpetually open character. The two-time Olympic gold medal winner not only consistently refused to join a club but also to accept invitations to compete. It would be reasonable to speculate that had he been blessed with the patience, discipline, and fortitude which other athletes of his caliber possessed, Fuchs would have dominated fencing as completely and for as long as Weisz did heavyweight wrestling. Fuchs's peculiar behavior, however, did not adversely affect the performance of other Jewish fencers. In fact his aloofness helped them to make their mark more easily and quickly on the "nation of fencers." In the individual foil competition only one Jew, Dezső Földes, managed to win a national championship (1910). József Brachfeld and József Fodor helped the Nemzeti Vívó Club to capture the national title in 1914. In the individual épée competition, the years just preceding the First World War were dominated by Lajos Werkner, Fuchs's teammate on the 1908 and 1912 gold medal winning Hungarian Olympic team. He won three consecutive national titles (1912-14) and was a member of the Nemzeti Vívó Club.

Enthusiasm ran high among the first generation of Jewish athletes in Hungary to tame the velocipede, that "wire donkey" of still cumbersome construction, airless tires, and high rimless wheels, which became the center of public fascination in the last decades of the nineteenth century. At first the velocipede was fair game. Anyone with courage, decent leg muscles, and firm buttocks attempted to coax speed out of its bumpy forward progress. Among the earliest aficionados were such luminaries as the champion gymnast Dávid Müller and Lajos Tótisz, the best long jumper of his time. Soon, however, Jewish athletes made an undivided commitment to competitive cycling and achieved notable results. Hermann A. Schwartz was a champion cyclist as well as one of the founders of the Budapest Cycling Club. Nándor Dreilinger, Márton Frisch, and Artúr Löwy were national champions in 1900, 1901, and 1903 respectively. Samu Símó, Dezső Spitz, Salamon Deutsch, Béla Schwab and Nándor Velvárt won numerous national and international races, laying the foundation of a strong Jewish presence in the prewar history of cycling in Hungary.

The participation of Jews in ice-skating was more a result of emulating the Hungarian nobility than the consequence of curiosity in anything introduced from abroad. Ice-skating, it is recalled, was the only one of the social sports which Budapest's elegant ladies and gentlemen took up with increasing enthusiasm. Thus for the capital's Jewry, for whom socially upward mobility was an important byproduct of assimilation, ice-skating became a preferred pastime. Located in the middle of Városliget, Budapest's sprawling and picturesque park, a large lake served as the center of the growing popular infatuation with winter sports. Small flags were posted at tramway stops whenever the lake was safe for skating, prompting young men and women to dash for the ice.

Organized in 1869, the Budapest Korcsolyázó Egylet (*BKE,* "The Budapest Ice-Skating Club") was the principal means of transition from pastime to competition for every talented skater. (In fact, between 1900 and 1949 *BKE* skaters won all national championships in both men's and women's speed and figure skating.) Skill and grace rather than speed and endurance seemed to be the qualities in ice-skating that attracted the earliest Jewish competitors to the sport. There is no evidence in the record books of achievements by Jewish speed skaters. The extant statistical data from the prewar period of figure skating, however, tells a different tale. Árpád Weisz won the first national championship in 1900 and Jenő Márkus placed first in 1903. Between 1908 and 1922 the Hungarian national championship was indisputably a Jewish monopoly.

It was during the first three years of this period that a most genuinely remarkable accomplishment was recorded by a Jewish woman. Until 1924 men and women competed together in figure skating national championships, so that when in 1908 Lili Kronberger became champion of Hungary and retained the title for two consecutive years, she proved herself against both sexes. Her quest for international fame began in 1906 when she placed second in the world championship in Davos. Next year in Vienna she again finished in second place. However in 1908 Kronberger captured the world championship held in Tropau and remained the world's best figure skater for three more years (1909 Budapest, 1910 Berlin, and 1911 Vienna). Kronberger also significantly influenced the future course of ice-skating. It is said that she was the first figure skater to successfully complete an entire program with musical accompaniment.

Kronberger's lock on the national championship was broken by Andor Szende, who won the title in 1911 and did not relinquish it until 1923. He was a talented athlete both on and off the ice. As a long jumper Szende left a trail of well-earned victories. Although he exceeded Kronberger's record of national titles, in international competition Szende fell far short of his female counterpart's achievement. Not that he did not try. Between 1910 and 1914 he compiled an enviable record against the best figure skaters of his time. Yet top honors consistently eluded him in both world and European championships. He placed third, fourth, and fifth in world championships in 1910, 1911, and 1914 respectively. In European championships he reversed the sequence of his world championship performance, finishing fifth in St. Petersburg in 1911, but in 1913 capturing second place in Kristiania, his best showing in international competition.

Although Hungarians were relative latecomers in the initial phase of the development of table tennis—Britain, Russia, and India all claimed to have originated the sport—they would become enthusiastic, permanent devotees. In 1902, three years after table tennis took root in England, the sport was introduced in Budapest. Table tennis soon became a Jewish monopoly and until the outbreak of the Second World War it may justifiably be characterized as a Hungarian-Jewish sport.

Sport? Surely no one would dignify by that title a pastime that is also called ping-pong, a game played out of boredom wherever a table, a celluloid ball, and a couple of paddles are found, and which offers no more strenuous physical exercise than the continuous bending down and straightening out required by the search for the ball and its retrieval from under the furniture. It was already a major victory for this stepchild of sports when tennis players—they were after all its first aficionados—languishing in an enforced seasonal hiatus, began calling it winter tennis and played spirited matches in loosely organized and sparsely attended quasi-championships.

Predictably, the earliest Hungarian experience in competition was rather embarrassing. The Austrian Ervin Kaufmann, and Edward Shires, an English engineer living in Budapest, dominated the first competition in 1904. By the following year, however, the Hungarians made great strides in improving their game. They took charge of the national championship, beating Kaufmann and Shires. The first world championship was held in 1922, but European players had to wait until 1958 to compete for the continental titles. Olympic recognition eluded table tennis altogether. The slow development of the international organizational structure of the sport kept the prewar players from gaining valuable experience and fostered an inbreeding of technique and style. Also, the first Hungarian players, the so-called wood-surface paddle generation, were more adversely affected by the immediate pre- and postwar conditions than those in other sports.

Between 1912 and 1925 no national competition was held. The domination of Jewish players and of the *MTK* began when Dezső Freund, with a non-Jewish teammate, Albert László, won Hungary's first national doubles championship. Through the rest of the prewar years only one doubles title (1909) was won without the help of at least one Jewish teammate. Zoltán Mechlovits won in 1910 and 1911; Zoltán Székely in 1912.

One of the greatest champions of Hungary was Zoltán Mechlovits of the *MTK*. He was able to extend his career in competition to nearly two decades, forming a bridge between the pre-1914 period when the standard of the game and the quality of the players still suffered from the lack of international matches, and the interwar years, when the establishment of national and international associations at long last assured table tennis the recognition and means of development that had been sought since the turn of the century. Mechlovits represented a new breed of players, whose commitment to table tennis was unswerving. He won only one national singles championship (1911) in the prewar era. Mechlovits teamed up with the non-Jewish Roland Jacobi—then both members of the *MTK*—and won the national doubles championship in 1910 and 1911.

The last great Jewish *MTK* player to exert a dominating influence in the shadow of the war was Dániel Pécsi. A physician by profession, Pécsi won the last prewar national singles championship in 1912. Although an outstanding doubles player as well, he could not duplicate Mechlovits's feat. In the year of his victory in the singles competition, the doubles title was won by the *MTK* team of Zoltán Székely and the non-Jewish Gusztáv Nádasi.

No sport revealed the Jews' assimilationist ambitions as much as soccer. This was the sport that also provided the largest non-Jewish segment of Hungary's population, concentrated at one place weekend after weekend, the opportunity to watch and react to the performance of Jewish players. By no means an accurate test of the degree of popular acceptance of the

Jews, soccer nonetheless exposed Jewish players to the most careful scrutiny by the largest group of spectators in the most public of sports.

Predictably the results were inconclusive. Whereas social and religious prejudices surfaced only rarely, usually touched off by the emotional trauma of groups of undisciplined individuals reacting to a missed opportunity or a display of unsportsmanlike conduct, the public's acceptance of Jewish players and appreciation of their performance had no remedial effect on the traditional relations between Jew and Christian. Indeed at first glance soccer possessed none of the attributes that had attracted Jews to the other prewar sports. In theory, the inherent communality, subordinating individual initiative to group effort, and the downward social mobility which resulted in its soon becoming an object of frenzied adulation for the masses, ought to have made soccer unattractive to Jews, who were still somewhat apprehensive of the off-field manifestations of anti-Semitism which might so easily incite spectators at a match to violence. The sheer magic of the game, however, broke down theoretical obstacles and social barriers.

Hungarians came to the game relatively late. By 1896, when the Hungarian-born Charles Lányi-Löwenrosen, who had emigrated to England a few years earlier, returned to his native land and placed a ball on display at the Millennial Exhibition, the game had already nearly a three-thousand-year-long history. It started among the Chinese, who called it *tshu-chu,* or possibly even earlier in ancient Egypt. It enjoyed a virtually unbroken development in Greco-Roman times and medieval Europe. By 1891 most of the familiar characteristics of soccer (except for the offside rule which took effect in 1925) had evolved. Shinguards were first used in 1874; the referee's whistle first rang out in 1878; the first two-handed throw from out of bounds was executed in 1882; and in 1891 the first pair of net-backed goal posts made their appearance and the dreaded penalty was introduced.

That soccer should reach Hungary only after it had conquered the hearts of sportsmen in a score of other countries in Europe and overseas, leading to the development of organizational structure and the playing of international matches, was probably due to a combination of two sources of apprehension, one real and one imagined. Because of its rapidly growing mass appeal, soccer alienated the class-conscious traveling members of the nobility and upper bourgeoisie, the customary nineteenth-century import agents of sports, who believed that affluence, leisure, and play constituted a natural sequence and were the inalienable possessions of the privileged segments of society. Others were simply repelled by rumors. In 1894 Hungarian newspapers printed articles written by the opponents of soccer, who cited alarming albeit undocumented statistics. It was noted that in England in the previous three years 74 people lost their lives and 437 were injured and crippled playing soccer. The game must not be allowed to take root in Hungary, they concluded. Few people paid attention to the prophets of doom. No more successful were the efforts of some members of Parliament, who declared that soccer was "a sport for wild men" and tried to introduce legislation banning it. The ball rolled over the objections of apprehensive elitists and became the symbol of all sports for the largest segment by far of Hungary's sport-loving people.

Predictably there was enthusiasm for soccer among Jewish athletes. Like their non-Jewish counterparts, they eagerly responded to any new, physically challenging activity. However, the foundations of the future popularity of soccer among Jews were laid not on the field but in the small public parks and on patches of vacant land where children gathered to play impromptu matches and where the career of many a would-be player started. Of the most popular playgrounds—some bearing informal names that remained a source of nostalgia for generations who grew up around them—two were in the centers of districts heavily populated by Jews. One was wedged in among large apartment buildings whose predominantly middle-class residents from 1869 to 1892 were represented in Parliament by Mór Wahrmann (1832-92), a noted financial expert and leader in industry as well as one of the most prominent members of the Jewish community of Pest, whose president he was for a decade until his death. The other was the "Grund," an undeveloped area around the Dohány Street Synagogue, the two-steepled neo-Moorish structure that was completed in 1859 and was the spiritual center of Hungary's Neolog Jews.

In keeping with the then-prevailing practice of multiple athletic involvement, many of the earliest generation of soccer players had already achieved notable success in the pursuit of other sports. One of the first Jewish athletes to succumb to the lure of soccer was Alfréd Hajós-Guttmann. The two-time gold medalist who swam at the 1896 Olympic Games quickly learned the rudiments of the game and was soon recognized as one of Hungary's top offensive players. He was selected for a variety of national teams. He was the inside left, his customary position, on the first Rambler team—made up of Budapest's best club players for a series of matches during the summer recess—that played its Viennese counterpart to a scoreless tie on 30 June 1900. He was tapped for a repeat performance against Britain's Surrey Wanderers (13 April 1901), the second of the two unofficial matches Hungary's national team played. Neither became a treasured topic in the fireside chats of oldtimers. Following a 4-0 thrashing from Richmond *AFC,* another British team, only two days earlier, the Hungarians again failed to rise to the occasion. Receiving only one goal, the Wanderers kicked five to Jakab Aschner, the Hungarian goalie who was the other Jewish player on the national team.

Aschner would not be given another chance to prove his abilities, but Hajós-Guttmann was allowed to remain at his position. He played inside left in the first official international match against Austria in Vienna. Unlike his highly successful swimming career, Hajós-Guttmann's association with Hungary's national soccer team was devoid of victories, although simply being chosen to play on the team was a victory of sorts. On 12 October 1902 the first official international match recorded by the Magyar Labdarúgó Szövetség ("Hungarian Soccer Federation") ended in defeat. In Vienna's famed Prater Stadium the Austrians invaded the Hungarians' goal five times and kept Hajós-Guttmann and his fellow strikers from scoring. However, success in the national championship may have provided him consolation. Hajós-Guttmann was a member of the soccer team of the Budapest Torna Club, which captured first place in the first two national championships (1901 and 1902), when only teams from the capital competed. The winner was also awarded the title of Champion of Budapest. After he retired from active play, Hajós-Guttmann was appointed selector-manager of the national team. Only belatedly were his efforts crowned with success. On 5 November 1906 in Budapest's Millenáris Stadium Hajós-Guttmann's team defeated Austria's national eleven by a score of 3-1. An earlier match, the only previous victory against the favorite foe was an untypical test of talents due to an unresolved controversy in the Austrian Soccer Federation as a result of which players of the Vienna and Cricketter teams withdrew and the Austrians even had to borrow a Hungarian player, Herquett of the *MTK,* to bring their team to full strength. After the match, Hajós-Guttmann resigned his position.

He was to witness another Hungarian victory in the surprising capacity of referee. At the dawn of international matches the principal considerations in the selection of referees were availability and knowledge of the rules of the game, not third-country neutrality. On 7 April 1907 in the Millenáris Stadium Hajós-Guttmann refereed an international match between Hungary and Bohemia that ended with Hungary's 5-2 victory.

By virtue of his Olympic victories Hajós-Guttmann was the best-known Jewish athlete playing soccer in the prewar period. The steadily growing popularity of the game, however, was bound to attract many Jewish athletes from other sports. Out of their ranks emerged some of Hungary's best-known and most popular players, who performed to the delight—and occasionally to the chagrin—of an ever-growing band of loyal and enthusiastic fans. They represented Hungary in international matches and a variety of clubs in the national divisions.

Even though anti-Semitism affected virtually all walks of life in varying degrees of intensity, it did not create a stumbling block in the path of the steadily advancing career of Jewish players. The occasionally abusive catcalls made by those fans who were impervious to even a modicum of sensitivity and propriety were an innate part of the game, something all players have to endure.

In no other sport does the lack of reliable information concerning the religious affiliation of athletes present a greater hindrance to the identification of Jewish players than in soccer. Despite the inevitable risk of doing an injustice to many a Jewish soccer player whose statistics are preserved in Hungarian record books and are thus available to those who are interested, this study cannot pretend to catalog them all. Because of the popularity of soccer a strictly quantitative list of Jewish players who were active in the period ending in 1918 would be impractically lengthy, besides being predictably incomplete. The dream and ultimate goal of every soccer player, as well as the most convincing sign of recognition by the technical leadership and a virtual guarantee for enduring popularity with the fans, is being tapped for Hungary's national team. Approximately thirty Jewish players, mostly members of the *MTK* and the *FTC*, the two most popular clubs, represented Hungary in international matches between 1901 and 1918.

As a real service to the gossip-prone, to those who enjoy statistics of all sorts, especially bits and pieces about players, performance, goals, and

so forth, knowledgeable contributors to the history of soccer often provide detailed information about the players who became members of the
"golden team" of a specific period. Though undoubtedly arbitrary—some
players who represented Hungary in international matches are routinely
excluded—and a source of never-ending controversy, the selection does
provide an opportunity for everyone to name his best of the best. Even
though the lengthy careers of some players result in overlap, the purists
favor the fractionation of chronology and minute accuracy of detail. They
tend to divide the decades before 1920 into three distinct periods and set
up a "golden team" for each. They also identify the most outstanding
players, who, because of the inherent limitations the best eleven imposes
on the selection procedure, were left out, yet whose excellences ought to
be recognized. The names of Jewish players would soon appear on the lists
of every knowledgeable selector, armchair or professional.

Though he was not one of the "immortals" of the first period (1902-
5), one Jewish player captured the attention of both professional chroniclers and knowledgeable fans. Ferenc Weisz is remembered as the first
genuine all-round soccer player in Hungary who in the course of an unforgettable, seventeen-year-long career (beginning in 1902) took full
advantage of the then-rare ability to use both feet with equal facility. He
played the full spectrum of positions, from goalie to outside left. A
pharmacist by profession, Weisz played for his beloved *FTC* 382 times,
kicking 192 goals, and represented Hungary in seventeen international
matches. Youthful enthusiasm and an energy that helped him to remain
among the best after most of his contemporaries had retired, were qualities which coaches strove to instill in many a generation of youthful
players.

Most knowledgeable aficionados pay special tribute to the second
golden age, which lasted from 1906 to 1914. In the wake of visiting
English teams, soccer in Hungary matured and a new generation of players, fully trained in technique and skills, took to the field. The teams were
at full strength, since the luring away of outstanding players tempted by
lucrative foreign contracts still had not begun, so the fans were treated
to exciting matches. Because of the emergence of an inordinately large
number of outstanding players, the second period is often divided into
two parts—from 1906 to 1911 and from 1911 to 1914—to allow for a
greater overview. Each had its "golden team" and coterie of famous

players who, though they did not make the team, played head and shoulders above their contemporaries. Unlike the "golden team" of the first period, which contained not a single Jewish player (Ferenc Weisz was only recognized as one of the top players, but his versatility may have sidetracked the selectors of the "golden team" and led them to tap other players who consistently performed in one position), the second period revealed the presence of a surprisingly large number of Jewish players. In the "golden team" of the first half of the period there actually were more Jewish than non-Jewish players. Playing left back, Oszkár Szendrő (Schwartz) of the *BTE* was considered the best at the position throughout most of the prewar period. A calm and dependable defender, Szendrő is remembered for his great speed, flawless defensive skills both in the air and on the ground, and sportsmanlike conduct. Between 1908 and 1911 he was tapped for Hungary's national team thirteen times. His only shortcoming is said to have been a willingness to resort to the kind of aggressive play with which many defenders hope to intimidate goal-hungry strikers.

The presence of Jewish players was particularly felt in the midfield. Playing on the right side, Gyula Bíró of the *MTK* was considered one of the greatest Hungarian players of all times. He was only sixteen years old when he played his first international match for Hungary. He was to be accorded this ultimate recognition of excellence thirty-six times between 1906 and 1916. His style, the experts and fans agree, was ahead of his time, reminiscent of midfielders decades later. A player of unique physical and cerebral qualities, Bíró possessed a seemingly inexhaustible reservoir of energy and a proclivity for brilliant, often witty, technical maneuvers that confused his opponents and delighted the fans. He helped out on defense, launched his strikers on attack with passes he executed with mathematical accuracy and frequently threatened the goalies of opposing teams with powerful shots from great distances. Bíró's commanding presence on the field successfully concealed his relative lack of speed, which is generally held to have been his sole weakness.

No position in soccer carries a heavier burden of responsibility than that of the sweeper. He is the pillar of the defense, whose performance can make or break a team. The honor of playing that position in the "golden team" of the 1906-11 years was shared by Sándor Bródy of the *FTC* and the non-Jewish Jenő Károly of the *MTK*. Unlike Bíró, Bródy is remembered not for the unsurpassed brilliance of his play, but for his diligence, endurance, enthusiasm, and dependability. Though of medium height, the muscular and agile Bródy dominated the airspace in front of the goal with his authoritative head play, an activity to which some of his admirers goodnaturedly attributed his premature balding. For the *FTC*, whose old-time fans recall his engaging personality and commanding presence on the field with unflagging reverence, he played 307 first-division matches and scored seventeen goals, helping it to win fourteen national championships. He represented Hungary in seventeen international matches.

Like his counterpart on the right, Antal Vágó (Weisz) was the selectors' unanimous choice for left midfielder. If he had a weakness no one seems to be able to remember it. Flawless ball control, accurate passing, unerring instinct for being at the right place at the right time and an astonishing range of defensive skills were the most often cited characteristics of this complete player. He complemented Bíró perfectly. When Bíró plunged into offensive plays Vágó fell back to provide cover against possible counterattack. This smooth and efficient midfield pair was one of the strongest components of the Hungarian national teams, in which Vágó played seventeen times.

Being Jewish and belonging to the *MTK* were characteristics the two players on the right side of the forward line of this "golden team" shared with the midfielders. Lightning speed, imaginative dribbling, and accurate passing, qualities that all great wingers possess, were typical of Béla Sebestyén's style. The popular right winger terrorized the defense of opposing teams. His only weakness may be deduced from the statistical data available. Wingers of Sebestyén's ability were not only indispensable ingredients in the preparation of attacks, they also frequently were the executors. However, scoring goals was not one of Sebestyén's notable skills. In the course of a distinguished career he played on Hungary's national team twenty-four times between 1906 and 1912. Yet he kicked only two goals, an unusually low figure. He is remembered as an exceedingly unselfish player who frequently broke through the defense yet invariably passed the ball to a teammate, preferring to remain in the periphery while others scored the goals.

Though Sebestyén is often thought of in the company of the non-Jewish Sándor Bodnár, a dangerous inside right who between 1910 and 1916 appeared twenty times among Hungary's national eleven and scored twenty goals, many selectors paired him with Vilmos Kertész II, the inside right of the *MTK*. The most famous of three Jewish brothers of the *MTK*— Gyula was a center forward who played only once for Hungary and Adolf, a left midfielder, was an eleven-time international—Vilmos eventually moved back to midfield, where after playing on the left side he switched to the right and became Gyula Bíró's heir. Between 1910 and 1924 Kertész II was called on to play for Hungary forty-seven times. He scored eleven goals. His rise to the top had been meteoric, one of the most astounding in the history of Hungarian soccer. In the course of two months in 1909 he advanced from the third team of the *MTK* into the national eleven, whose pillar he would remain for a decade and a half. He was a quick, intelligent, powerful player whose technical skills were a source of be-fuddlement to the defenders of opposing teams. A jovial man on and off the field, Kertész II was a popular favorite of fans, who delighted in his often devilishly witty dribbling—which, however, occasionally backfired, causing moments of anxiety to his teammates. Wrote one journalist in the twilight of the great Jewish player's career: "Kertész II is like a noble vine. The older the better." It is remembered that Kertész II gave his most memorable performance in a match against Austria on 23 September 1923, when he was thirty-three. Experts and fans agree the match, which Hungary won 2-0, was one of the most exciting and enjoyable in the long history of meetings between the two central European rivals.

In the second "golden team" (1911-14) of the period only two Jewish players, Gyula Bíró and Béla Sebestyén, were repeaters. They had no equals. The third, a newcomer, Zoltán Blum of the *FTC,* was a popular and unanimous choice. Unlike Vágó and Kertész II, with whom he at first alternated as the left midfielder on the national team and whose heir he eventually became, Blum was not a player who dazzled opponents with a brilliant display of technical skills. The slender, soft-spoken young man who was to serve his team for nearly a decade was an indefatigable work-horse. He played an astounding 416 matches for the *FTC* and subsequent-ly became a much-loved and respected coach. From beginning to end he played with enthusiasm and determination, reliably anticipating the often unpredictable course of the ball. He was a commanding presence in the air, where his headers figured decisively on defense and in the prepara-tion of attacks. Even though Blum never managed to correct the major flaws of his style—he was an excessive "lefty" and his passing was far from accurate—the selectors of the national eleven tapped him thirty-eight times.

The makeup of the "golden team" of the war years revealed yet another upsurge of Jewish players. Kertész II the popular midfielder and striker of the *MTK* was the only repeater among the players of the previous "golden team." In addition, three other Jewish players were selected.

Up until the end of the First World War only one Jewish player was thought to deserve to be included in the elite company of outstanding goalies. Miksa Knapp, the lanky, courageous, and ubiquitous goalkeeper of the *MTK*, won recognition of his talents at a time when the legendary Károly Zsák, who has generally been described as the greatest Hungarian goalie of all times, virtually monopolized that most decisive of defensive positions. Alternating with Zsák, Knapp became an eight-time member of Hungary's national team between 1914 and 1917. He is remembered with respect and gratitude for greatly contributing to the initial phase of a remarkable series of victories which made the *MTK* the champion of Hungary's first division ten consecutive times (1915-1924). The talented Knapp died at 28 in 1918, in the prime of his playing career, a victim of Spanish influenza.

Adolf Kertész III played eleven times on the national team between 1911 and 1920. The youngest of the three talented Kertészes of the *MTK* won the nod from the selectors of the "golden team" of the war years. The statistics in his case are deceiving. For the left midfielder's position he competed against such outstanding players as Vágó, Blum, and Kertész II. His playing skills impressed experts and fans alike. Though hampered by a weakness in one arm, Kertész III's style was effortless and his technique flawless. Pinpoint accuracy of passing and unerring instinct in checking were his most memorable assets, making him a key player on both offense and defense. His death in 1920 at age twenty-eight ended a brilliant career. He was the victim of a car accident in Saarbrücken, where he had settled only a few months earlier.

Following closely in the footsteps of Kertész II, his teammate in the *MTK*, was Imre Tauszig. Possessing great speed and a flair for imaginative dribbling and for accurately centering the ball, Tauszing, known affectionately by his nickname, "Böske," was the best outside right in Hungary between 1914 and 1919 even though he was tapped for the national team only five times. It is recalled that Tauszig had great difficulty keeping his nerves under control and was forced to take tranquilizers regularly before matches.

The selection of players for the "golden team" reflects a fusion of emotion and pragmatism that appears arbitrary but in fact can be justified. However, the inherent limitations of naming the eleven best players of any period have been the cause of heated debates, frustration, and disappointment as many a favorite went untapped. Some received the consolation of seeing their heroes chosen for the national team. Although it was less exclusive and changed more frequently than the "golden team," the national eleven was, after all, an elite group. The selectors' intricate considerations of individual ability and skill and their efforts to take the broad framework of team priorities into account dashed the hopes of many excellent club players who were either never selected or only chosen once or twice.

Similarly, there were outstanding Jewish players who, though excluded from the "golden teams," contributed much to the development of soccer in Hungary and made an indelible impression on generations of grateful fans and discriminating officials. They played for a variety of teams, generally in Budapest and mostly for the *MTK*, and often stood in the limelight as a result of excellent performance in weekend divisional matches but were seldom tapped for the national eleven.

In the pre-1918 Hungarian national teams the presence of Jewish players, a tradition that began with the first international match played by Hungary, was a virtually foregone conclusion. An outstanding feature of the makeup of the national eleven was the upward fluctuation of numbers. For example, five Jewish players—Szendrő, Bíró, Bródy, Vágó, and Sebestyén—helped Hungary down its archrival, Austria, by a score of 5-3 in Budapest on 1 November 1908. With Kertész II's quick rise to fame as the best Hungarian inside right there actually were more Jewish than non-Jewish players on the national team that edged Austria 4-3 in Vienna on 2 May 1909. That remarkable statistic was not an isolated phenomenon, not simply one of the quirks of sporting life. The influx of Jewish players into the national team for the rest of the pre-1919 period, continuing through the interwar years, remained a unique feature of Hungarian soccer. The supply was readily available and the selectors drew from a steadily growing pool of outstanding Jewish players. The Hungarian national team that on 3 June 1917 trounced Austria 6-2 contained six Jewish

players, five of whom—Knapp, Feldmann, Kertész III, Blum, and Weisz—
had never played on that team before. Only Kertész II, the sixth player,
was a repeater.

In conclusion, the contributions of three other Jewish players must be
recognized. Between 1907 and 1911 Izidor Kürschner, the left midfielder
of the *MTK*, played five times for Hungary in international matches.
Though physically unimpressive—he is remembered as actually being in-
capable of kicking the ball forcefully—the popular Dóri was a model of
reliability and simplicity, virtues at odds with the flashy, crowd-pleasing
style that marked the careers of many of his contemporaries. They, however, found that playing against Kürschner was an exasperating experience.
He possessed an unerring sense for positioning himself, headed the ball
accurately and with authority, and played indefatigably.

Unlike the unprepossessing Kürschner, Béla Révész struck fear in the
hearts of strikers by his mere presence. The huge, powerfully built right
back of the *MTK* often proved an immovable obstacle in the path of
skillfully woven attacks. What he lacked in agility and speed he made up
with an enviable ability to use both feet with destructive aplomb (in those
days most players dribbled, passed and shot with one foot exclusively).
He also was known for his good, though not outstanding, headers. According to the recollections of his teammates, Révész trained harder and longer
than anyone. His diligence and discipline paid handsome dividends. Between 1909 and 1915 he spearheaded Hungary's defense eight times.

Few of the sharp-eyed followers of Hungarian soccer detected even a
single shortcoming in ability or a flaw in technique when Révész's heir,
Gyula Feldmann, betook himself to the field. He was the quintessential
defender, hard-playing, intelligent, and inventive. His predisposition to
be at the right place at the right time, his superb kicking technique, and
his composure under pressure made him a much-respected member of
three clubs (*NSC, FTC*, and *MTK*) he successively played for, as well as
the national team for which he was selected ten times between 1910 and
1920. Feldmann was the first in Hungary who successfully used the
sliding tackle, one of the most effective methods of separating ball and
player.

Since its introduction, soccer in Hungary attracted more devoted and
knowledgeable fans than all other sports combined. They followed the
careers of players they loved to love and players they loved to hate in

unabashed frenzy and committed to memory a staggering multiplicity of plays, goals scored, and shots saved. In the hope of soothing the justifiably ruffled sensitivies of the reader who may be just one such fan, shaking his head and muttering, "Ah, he should have made mention of __," let the following be said in the spirit of commiseration and apology. Every fan has favorites among players past and present and will swallow hard, suppressing bitter feelings, whenever the talents of favorites go unrewarded. The task of giving recognition to Jewish soccer players was no less difficult than that of, let's say, the selector of a club or a national team. There is only so much space to a book; there are only so many positions to a team. Let the intent of collective remembrance act as assuagement.

CHAPTER III

PLAYING THE GAME IN THE ADMIRAL'S KINGDOM

As the outbreak of the First World War sent its destructive ripples across Europe a surge of patriotic fervor gripped the hearts of people. For Jews everywhere the war presented a unique opportunity to display their loyalty as citizens and participate in all phases of the war effort. The public image of Jews—middle-class, professional, mercantile, and cultured—received a dramatic extension into a realm not generally associated with Jewish life. Their emergence as a wartime people was a predictable consequence of the steady course of assimilation acknowledged by parliamentary legislation that placed them on equal footing with their non-Jewish countrymen.

Hungarian Jews responded to the manifold challenges of the war with enthusiasm and determination. They fought on the battlefield, received promotions and decorations, and elicited expressions of praise from some of the highest-ranking officers in the Austro-Hungarian army, who cited the bravery of Jewish soldiers and paid tribute to the nearly ten thousand Jews who died the death of heroes. They attended to the needs of the wounded—the majority of army doctors were Jewish—and contributed to the uninterrupted flow of war materiel. They pledged millions of crowns in war loans.

The defeat of the Central Powers had a devastating effect on the imperial institutions. The disintegration of the Dual Monarchy, ending the rule of the Habsburgs, signaled the dawn of the new age for which Hungarians had been waiting since the dismal failure of the Revolution of 1848. One of the last official acts of the last Habsburg emperor, Charles IV, in his capacity as a king of Hungary, was to appoint on 1 November 1918 a coalition government headed by Count Mihály Károlyi, leader of the opposition in Parliament. The Károlyi government, however, proved short-lived. It was rendered ineffective by its own administrative and political inexperience, the lack of a supporting national organization, the increasing decentralization of political power, and the growth of opposition. On 24 November 1918 the Communist Party of Hungary was founded. Its leaders made use of the *Vörös Újság* ("Red Gazette"), the official organ of the party, to initiate a political offensive that also involved the implementation of a four-point program: establishment of an efficient party organization; recruitment of workers, peasants, disaffected ex-soldiers, and radical intellectuals; dissemination of propaganda, and general mobilization. Within five months the Communists managed to wreck the precarious structure of Hungary's postwar political system. Modeled on the Russian precedent and drawing inspiration from Lenin's encouragement, the Hungarian-Soviet Republic came into being on 21 March 1919.

Distinctive characteristics of the long-range impact of the emancipation of the Jews and their assimilation into European society were the speed, determination, and enthusiasm with which they adopted virtually all forms and expressions of their new, unfettered condition. No direct result of this process has been debated more heatedly or received more adverse publicity than the relationship of Jews to Communism. Communists of Jewish origin never quite succeeded in shaking off their religious heritage despite their ideological convictions. To their coreligionists on the right of the political spectrum they became a source of never-ending bewilderment and embarrassment; to anti-Semites they were the agents of Judeo-Bolshevism, another manifestation of conspirational and subversive activity with which Jews threatened the structure of Christian society. In few countries did Jews give more support to such disparate forms of political reaction or more ammunition to the propaganda of conservatism and the defenders of the old regime than in Hungary. Eight of the twenty-member anti-Habsburg National Council of Count Mihály Károlyi were Jews. The percentage grew higher as the rapid succession of events pushed Hungary in the direction of Communism. Of the thirty People's Commissars of the Hungarian-Soviet Republic seventeen were of Jewish origin. Hungarian Jewry would derive no immediate or long-range benefits as a consequence of this dramatic interlude. The mostly middle-class Jews were suspect in the eyes of the Communist leadership, which ordered the execution of forty-four Jews accused of counterrevolutionary activity. In the anti-Communist interwar regime of Admiral Miklós Horthy the Judeo-Bolshevik theme often resurfaced from the reservoir of anti-Jewish arguments. In the Hungarian People's Republic, established after the Second World War, Jewish origin was either a matter of pretended indifference or a factor in party purges.

Throughout their brief and ill-fated dictatorship, the leaders of the Hungarian-Soviet Republic desperately tried to maintain the impression of normality, stability, and success. Their ambitious slogans and sweeping decrees, aimed at transforming Hungary into a paradise of proletarians and progressive-minded peasants, created only an illusion, a precariously brittle façade that would soon start to crack and eventually crumble under the weight of reality. The unresolved bickering between Socialists and Communists, fratricidal disputes among the Communists, the ever-present threat posed by unvanquished counterrevolutionary groups, and the menacing stance of foreign anti-Communist forces were obstacles which the leaders of the Hungarian-Soviet Republic found insurmountable. Still, the illusion had to be sustained as long as the steadily constricting circumstances permitted it. Sport and physical education, opiates of the masses in times of turmoil and uncertainty, received much attention and support and were pressed into serving the goals of a cultural revolution. The sport associations of workers were charged with the difficult task of leadership. Only a progressive new generation of Hungarians, developing both physically and mentally, could fulfill the goals set by the Communist party.

Communists of Jewish origin bore much of the responsibility for reaching those goals. Dezső Bíró, who in 1905 was one of the founders and the president of the Munkás Testedző Egylet (*MTE*, "Workers' Physical Training Association"), was appointed to a five-member Directory of Physical Education Affairs, formed to oversee the reorganization of sports, and was subsequently elected its president. Fülöp Grünhut, a former copresident of the *MTE*, was also a member. Tibor Szamuely, Deputy People's Commissar of War, was one of the most active and vocal advocates of mass participation in sports. Tibor Fischer, by then a four-time heavyweight national wrestling champion, was selected to be the model for the hammer-wielding man, the symbol of Communism, that was imprinted on slogan-bearing posters and medals by which the government of the Hungarian-Soviet Republic goaded the populace to action and tried to sustain revolutionary fervor. Alfréd Hajós-Guttmann, the two-time Olympic swimming champion and a talented architect, was commissioned to draw up plans for refurbishing and expanding existing sports facilities, for an enclosed pool, and for the National Stadium. István Grosz of the *MTK* was the winner of the national cross-country run, finishing ahead of eighty-five competitors. Dr. Leó Donáth, a former national swimming champion on short distances, taught swimming to prospective physical education teachers.

No sports event left a more lasting and vivid impression in the annals of Communist Hungary than the sole international soccer match that Hungary played against Austria in "Red Budapest" on 6 April 1919. Ignoring the blockade that anti-Communist forces had set up around Hungary, the Austrian team received a huge ovation from 40,000 fans, the largest number on record to date. Accompanied by a rousing rendition of the "Marseillaise," political dignitaries and members of the Directory of Physical Education Affairs appeared and made speeches. The red-shirted national team of the Hungarian-Soviet Republic contained two Jewish players: Kertész II and József Braun, both of the *MTK*. The number could have been higher. Antal Vágó of the *MTK*, the outstanding left midfielder of his time, and Gyula Feldmann also of the *MTK*, who was the pillar of the Hungarian defense, chose not to play. Hungary won the match 2-1, the winning goal being scored by Braun. He was the newest link in a chain of Jewish players who had virtually monopolized the position of outside right since the turn of the century. (Braun's predecessors were Ferenc Braun of the *FTC*, Béla Sebestyén of the *MTK*, Ferenc Weisz of the *FTC*, Imre Tauszig of the *MTK*, József Winkler I of the *MTK*, and Sándor Nemes-Neufeld of the *FTC*.)

Notable individual achievements in sports in the course of the short-lived Hungarian-Soviet Republic were few and overshadowed by the efforts to draw the masses into physical education and sports. The nationalization of stadiums and other sports facilities, the organization of sports

in the Hungarian Red Army and among workers and peasants, the introduction of reforms aimed at the overhaul of the system of physical education in the schools, and the acceptance of plans aimed at the construction
of additional sports facilities were the most notable achievements of
the architects of the new order. Under the increasing weight of seemingly
irremediable domestic problems and the steadily mounting military pressure by Hungarian and foreign counterrevolutionary groups, the structure of the Hungarian-Soviet Republic crumbled. On August 1 the Revolutionary Governing Council and the Communist Party Executive
resigned. A caretaker government of trade unionists was formed. It func-
tioned for a mere six days, during which, however, it managed to dis-
mantle the edifice of Communist rule. On August 6 a counterrevolutionary
government, which had been operating in Szeged since May 19, took
over. But the real power was in the hands of groups of counterrevolutionary army officers, aided by Czech and Romanian troops. On November 16,
on a white horse, Admiral Miklós Horthy, commander of the counterrevolutionary army, made his official entry into Budapest.

The rule of the Communists was over but not forgotten. Horthy and
his army officers proved to be as merciless in liquidating the vestiges of
the Hungarian-Soviet Republic and punishing its supporters as the Communists had been in their zeal to send the old regime into oblivion. Little
difference in action may be discerned between the Lenin Boys—gangs
of convicts and other anti-social elements who terrorized the trapped
members of the former privileged classes—and the detachments of anti-
Communist army officers, under the command of Pál Prónay and Gyula
Ostenburg, that tortured and murdered many proven or suspected Communists they had apprehended.

Ironically, though not unexpectedly, the Jews were again high on the
enemy list. The proponents of political anti-Semitism virtually institutionalized Judeo-Bolshevism as one of the principal and permanent movements threatening to destroy the national traditions and Christian values
of Hungarian society. Jews were accused of shirking their patriotic responsibility during the First World War: specifically, of attempting to under-
mine the morale and will of the people; supplying low-quality, often un-
usable war materiel; and failing to participate in the national struggle for
victory. The lack of patriotism, the anti-Semites charged, amply mani-
fested itself also during the short-lived Hungarian-Soviet Republic, among
whose leaders and supporters Jews could be found in large numbers.

The Jewish community would never find an effective antidote to these accusations. It was not for want of trying. A Committee of the Hungarian-Jewish War Archives was formed but failed to make a sufficient impresion with the documents it had collected in an effort to prove the manifold Jewish contributions to the war effort. The role of the Jews in the counter-revolutionary movement apparently also went unnoticed. Few Hungarians ever learned of or attributed lasting importance to the evidence documenting it. Yet the evidence was substantial and impressive. The first counterrevolutionary government, whose minister of justice was the Jewish Lajos Pálmai, was formed in Arad. Much of its administrative and propaganda budget came from contributions made and solicited by the Jewish residents of the city. When the counterrevolutionary government transferred its activity to Szeged (19 May 1919) Jews again proved valuable supporters. Without their financial and organizational support—they were especially active in the formation of the Anti-Bolshevik Committee, a clearing house for counterrevolutionary activities—members of the new national army could not have been fed, clothed, trained, and armed. Fifteen of the seventy-two counterrevolutionary officers who occupied the barracks in Szeged, thereby clearing the way for the transfer of the government to that city, were Jewish. Shortly after the fall of the Hungarian-Soviet Republic the leaders of Budapest's Jewry issued a proclamation denouncing Communism, severing ties with Communists of Jewish origin and reaffirming the patriotism of Jews throughout the country. However, neither the repeated and emphatic pronouncements of Jewish leaders nor the concern voiced by some of Hungary's most prominent churchmen could prevent the outbreak of the "White Terror," brutally violent anti-Jewish acts perpetrated by groups of counterrevolutionary army officers, allegedly conducting mopping-up operations against Communists between August 1919 and May 1920. Nor would such statements succeed in restoring full public confidence in the Jews. Though acts of outright violence subsided when Horthy, as regent of Hungary, consolidated his rule and sought international recognition by applying for membership in the League of Nations in 1922, anti-Semitism became one of the constant and most readily discernible features of the quarter-century-long Horthy era.

Sustained by only a fragile façade of civility and toleration, under which the strong undercurrents of irredentist nationalist-Christian feelings

and activities were all too noticeable, Hungary's Jewry slowly and carefully re-created a lifestyle of comfort, stability, and affluence on foundations that were on the whole largely make-believe. They resumed their
activity in virtually all sectors of the nation's economy, culture, and
sport, and prospered under the watchful eyes of the government. Horthy's
conservative political philosophy, though mindful of the utility of anti-
Semitism as a means of unifying the nation, envisaged as its principal
goal the rectification of the injustice which the "vengeful" Treaty of
Trianon (June 1920) had perpetuated against Hungary, depriving it of
nearly three-fourths of its prewar territory. Horthy's fear of Soviet Communism resulted in a cautious orientation toward the West, imposing on
him discipline and restraint in dealing with the unresolved Jewish Question. Though he often boasted of being the first anti-Semitic head of
state of his time, Horthy managed to keep the disparate Fascist factions
at bay.

Count István Bethlen, Horthy's hand-picked prime minister, was a
moderate and an Anglophile. Between 1921 and 1931 Bethlen succeeded
in laying the foundation of a peculiar political system and used parliamentary and constitutional means to create an illusion of stability and
gain a measure of international recognition by having Parliament ratify
the Treaty of Trianon. Small wonder that however menacing and uncertain, the future did not seem to bother Hungary's overconfident Jewry.
They fixed their gaze on the prevailing conditions, were heartened by
opportunities allowed them, and remained loyal to their assimilationist
and patriotic traditions. Few of them seemed to detect or pay attention
to the faint outlines of the Holocaust which in their no-win situation
should have been a cause for communal concern.

As before World War I, in no area of Jewish achievement were the harbingers of success more satisfying and well received than in sports. The
utility of talent and performance in the service of national interest outweighed that of the philosophy of right-wing groups, such as the *MOVE*
(Magyar Országos Véderő Egyesület, or "Hungarian National Defense
Force Association") and the Keresztény Magyar Sportliga ("Christian
Hungarian Sports League"), which tried to imbue Hungarian youth with
the spirit of racism and irredentism and assure the supremacy of the
Magyar race by separating "Christian and Jewish sports." A clear proof of
this may be found during the short-lived sports blockade from November

1919 to May 1921. At British and French initiatives, nations that had belonged to the defeated Central Powers were excluded from international competition. Hungary reacted with indignation and joined Austria and Germany in forming a counterblockade. Even then the increasing Fascist influence was hardly felt in sports. In the national soccer team, whose international matches were limited to Austria and Germany, there consistently were five or six Jewish players. The captain of the team was Kertész II, and Ferenc Weisz and Ármin Sebők at least once were members of the selection committee. Subsequently Hungary sought to regain international respectability and negotiated the normalization of sports relations with Italy and Britain. It also vowed to keep politics out of sports, a seemingly empty gesture in view of the steady and alarming proliferation of Fascist organizations. Remarkably, the promise was kept.

Notwithstanding these auspicious signs of initial success, Hungary suffered a severe setback in its efforts to win similar recognition from the International Olympic Committee. Not only was Budapest deprived of the right to host the 1920 Olympic Games, but Hungary, along with the rest of the former Central Powers and the Soviet Union, was notified that it would not even be allowed to participate in the first postwar Olympiad.

Neither Hungary's failure to return to the Olympic fold nor the ominous implications of the growing popularity of the Fascist *MOVE*, whose sports organization of nearly a hundred clubs became the largest in the country, nor the unsavory legacy of the Hungarian-Soviet Republic had an adverse effect on the return of Jewish athletes to competition. Between 1920 and 1924 they recorded numerous outstanding achievements. The following Jewish athletes became national champions: István Grosz (cross-country run, 1919; 5000 meters, 1924; 4 x 1500-meter relay, 1924); Béla Helfer (200-meter hurdle, 1919-21); Pál Steiner (5000-meter team run, 1920-21); Armand Magyar (Greco-Roman wrestling; bantamweight, 1924); Ödön Radvány (Greco-Roman wrestling: lightweight, 1920); Andor Szende (skating, 1922); József Szalai (gymnastics: combined, 1923; flying rings, 1924; horizontal bar, 1924; and springboard diving, 1922); János Garay (fencing: épée, 1923); Oszkár Gerde (team fencing: épée, 1922 and 1924); Sándor Gombos (team fencing: épée, 1924); Tibor Fazekas (water polo, 1919-22); Ernő Liebner (water polo, 1920-22); Zoltán Rudas (water polo, 1923); and István Sándor (water polo, 1923).

Of all sports, soccer continued to reveal the greatest concentration of Jewish players. The composition of the "golden team," in theory the ideal coming-together of the best and most popular players of a period, provides the most convincing supporting piece of evidence. Between 1919 and 1926 seven of its eleven members were Jews—an unprecedented phenomenon and an unsurpassed record in the history of soccer in Hungary. Only two of the seven—Kertész II and Blum—were repeaters.

Of the three Jewish players who monopolized the midfield positions Gábor Obitz was the only newcomer. He played for Hungary fifteen times, whereas Kertész II and Blum were selected forty-seven and thirty-eight times respectively. Though he would leave a less lasting impression on the national team than either of the other midfielders, the small-statured Obitz is remembered as a remarkably agile and technically flawless player. His courage and determination made him invaluable as a defender; his accurate passing and circumspect yet explosive moves figured prominently in the preparation of attacks. He was a truly international player. Statistics-conscious fans of the *FTC* recall that he played 267 games for the green-and-whites; sport-loving Jews in neighboring Czechoslovakia watched him play for the Maccabi Brno between 1923 and 1926.

The center, György Orth, the sole non-Jewish striker on the "golden team," was the greatest Hungarian soccer player of all time. He was already accustomed to being surrounded by Jewish players in the *MTK*, the team in which he spent his brilliant but tragically concluded career and whose entire forward line was selected into the best eleven of this period.

József Braun was regarded by many as the best Hungarian outside right of all time. The popular Csibi, a tall, well-built player, possessed skills that were invariably described in superlatives. His control of the ball both in the air and on the ground was textbook-perfect. When he was in possession of it the apprehensive defenders of the opposing teams could expect to be severely tested by a lightning-quick sprint along the sideline ending in the accurate centering of the ball, or a dazzling display of imaginative and clever dribbling. He also terrorized goalies with well-aimed headers and powerful shots. Although his career was cut short by a series of injuries—he was only twenty-five when he retired—Braun was a member of Hungary's national team twenty-seven times between 1918 and 1926.

The most frequent and immediate recipient of Braun's prodigious talents and the most consistent "feeder" of the speedy winger was György Molnár. The talented heir to Kálmán Konrád II, the fabled inside right of the *MTK* and the national team, Molnár nearly matched Braun's much-admired technique and style. He customarily refrained from making close contact and his occasional changing moods adversely affected his play. Molnár's greatest asset was an indefatigable mobility, in recognition of which his teammates bestowed on him the nickname "Hangya," or "ant." He covered the length and breadth of the field from the referee's initial whistle to the three whistles that indicate the end of the game. Between 1920 and 1927 Molnár played for Hungary in twenty-six international matches. His most memorable performance was against Italy on 6 April 1924. In front of 40,000 fans in Budapest, the by-then renowned Jewish right wing scored five goals in Hungary's 7-1 victory: Molnár scored a hat trick—three goals—and Braun scored twice. The most remarkable thing about this overwhelming Hungarian triumph was that all seven goals were scored by Jewish players; apart from the right wing, a goal was scored by by Zoltán Opata, the center, and another by József Eisenhoffer, the inside left.

Diminutive stature was the most visible common denominator of the Jewish players who formed the left wing of the "golden team" of 1919-26. Ferenc Híres-Hirzer, the explosively quick and graceful inside left, was a dazzling playmaker and a prolific scorer of goals. His adeptness at accurate passing, powerful shooting, and the initiating of imaginative attacks from either his position or that of the outside left delighted the fans of a decade (1922-32) and won him international fame. "Kicsi," or "little," as he was popularly called, also played for some time for the Maccabi Brno and in Italy, where his quick and elegant moves earned him the nickname "Gazelle." His consistently high-quality performance made him an invaluable asset to the Hungarian national team for which he was selected thirty-two times.

Had nature not conspired against him, Rudolf Jeny would certainly have become a goalie, a position that fascinated him throughout his brilliant career. However, the small-statured and determined player found his niche among the immortals of Hungarian soccer as an outside left. His speed, powerful shots, and ability to center the ball accurately earned him the devotion of fans, the respect of opponents, and the admiration of the selectors of Hungary's national teams, who between 1919 and 1925 tapped him nineteen times. His best performance, it is recalled, was against Switzerland in Budapest on 25 March 1925. Hungary won by a score of 5-0. Of the five goals, four were scored by Jewish players: two by Jeny and two by Molnár, who played inside left in that game. Jeny enjoyed great popularity off the field too. His sense of humor, pleasant tenor voice, and talent for declamation won him many friends among players and fans alike.

The last seven preprofessional years (the professional period began in 1926 and ended in 1934) produced more outstanding Jewish players who were not selected into the "golden team" than any other period in the history of Hungarian soccer. Few self-respecting fans would excuse the failure to mention at least some of them. Not even the non-Jewish Károly Zsák, considered by most the greatest Hungarian goalie, could entirely overshadow the two outstanding Jewish goalies of the period. A powerfully built, quick, and fearless defender of the goal of the *FTC* (322 times) and the national team (8 times), Ignác Amsel possessed an uncanny ability to catch. He was nicknamed "Pók," or "spider," for having a seemingly magnetic effect on shots fired at his goal. He was also good at batting the ball away. Lajos Fischer, the goalie of the *VAC*, the only all-Jewish team in Hungary, closely approximated Amsel's remarkable talents. Although short, he was not only dependable but also capable of acrobatic saves. Fischer guarded the goal of the national team nine times between 1924 and 1926. He might have had a much longer and more illustrious career had he not emigrated to the United States in 1926 at the age of twenty-four.

Fischer's success was partly due to the excellence of his teammate, Dezső Grosz II. He was the master of the ball both in the air and on the ground. Although he was regarded as one of the best left backs of his time—calmness, flawless technical and kicking skills, and great speed were his principal assets—he played in the shadow of the legendary non-Jewish József Fogl III, for whom he substituted twice on the national team between 1924 and 1926. He too emigrated to the United States in 1926. Henrik Nádler of the *MTK* suffered in comparison with Zoltán Blum of the *FTC*, the preeminent left midfielder of his time, but the slender Nádler's repertoire of imaginative moves earned him sufficient recognition to win him a place on the national team six times between 1924 and 1926.

Like Rudolf Jeny, his teammate, Zoltán Opata, a seventeen-time international, enjoyed great popularity on and off the field. He was a versatile player familiar with the intricacies and demands of all offensive positions, although his ability to pass and shoot with either foot made him a natural center who could set either wing of strikers in motion. His sole weakness —uncertain ball control in the air—was due to myopia, not a lack of skill. Opata's engaging personality, carefree lifestyle and reputation as a witty conversationalist, qualities not commonly found in soccer players, delighted generations of appreciative fans and headline-hungry sports journalists.

The misfortune of having to play in the shadow of Rudolf Jeny clouded the career of Árpád Weisz. The slightly built outside left of the Törekvés Soccer Club played a smart game. He pulled away from defenders in bursts of speed, avoided body contact, and centered the ball accurately. In 1922 and 1923 he was a six-time international, a notable achievement in view of Jeny's monopoly of the position on the national team. Similarly, Molnár and Híres-Hirzer's successive monopolies of the position of inside left had adversely affected the careers of József Eisenhoffer and Illés Spitz. Eisenhoffer, a convert to Judaism, had a brief, mercurial career. Although hampered by excessive reliance on his left foot for passing and shooting, he was a dynamic player and a prodigious goal-scorer. Between 1920 and 1924 he played for Hungary eight times, scoring seven goals. He scored all the goals in Hungary's victories over Sweden and France (28 October 1923 and 4 June 1924 respectively). As a member of the *FTC* in 1923 and 1924 he played only twenty-nine games but scored twenty-five goals, a remarkable achievement. Spitz, a tireless, superbly skilled and ingeniously crafty player, was equally adept at making his winger look good with passes of pinpoint accuracy and taking on defenders, who were often rendered helpless by his bewildering body fakes and dribbling. Goalies feared him even though he is not remembered for his powerful shots. He scored most of his goals from near the goal line, slapping the ball into the net, a unspectacular but profitable alternative for which he earned the derisive but respectful nickname, "Master of the Trudging Goals." He played in six international matches.

One is tempted to search for a pungent finish to the chronicle of this most successful period in the participation of Jews in Hungarian soccer. Obligingly, the record books provide the details of two games that are ideally suited for this purpose. On 6 April 1924 in Budapest, Hungary trounced Italy by a score of 7-1. Of the six Jewish players on the Hungarian national team, five—Braun, Molnár, Opata, Eisenhoffer, and Jeny—manned the entire forward line. Four of them, scored all of Hungary's seven goals. Molnár did a hat trick, Braun scored twice, and Eisenhoffer and Opata once. The composition of Hungary's national team that on 4 June 1924 in Le Havre edged France's best eleven 1-0 revealed an even more astounding evidence of the dense concentration of Jewish players. Except for Ferenc "Tigris" (Tiger) Kropacsek of the *MTK,* considered the most fearless goalie of all time, and the legendary Fogl brothers, all the other eight players were Jews. The scorer of the lone goal was József Eisenhoffer, the inside left.

Hungary's quest to regain the respect of the International Olympic Committee ended in success in May 1924, and the preparations for participation in the 1924 Olympic Games got under way. Despite the growing Fascist influence, Horthy's desire to keep improving Hungary's image safeguarded the continued participation of Jewish athletes. Their achievements in Paris were modest. Alfréd Hajós-Guttmann and Dezső Lauber jointly won the silver medal in architectural design (the gold was not awarded) and János Garay won the bronze medal in the individual saber competition. He was also a member of the second-place saber team. Ferenc Gerő ran the last leg of the 4 x 100-meter relay, placing Hungary fourth; and fifth-place finishers were Ödön Radvány in Greco-Roman featherweight wrestling and Tibor Fazekas, a member of the water polo team.

The most painful Hungarian memory of the Paris Olympics was caused by the performance of the much-praised soccer team. In the first round Hungary, fielding eight Jewish players, trounced Poland by a score of 5-0. Three members of the all-Jewish forward line scored all the goals: two apiece by Híres-Hirzer and Opata and one by Eisenhoffer. The Hungarians looked forward to playing their second-round opponents with great confidence. On 29 May 1924 eight thousand spectators watched an inspired Egyptian team take what to the eight Jewish players on the Hungarian team must undoubtedly have seemed a belated revenge for the biblical plagues. The Egyptian defenders shut out the all-Jewish Hungarian forward line—Braun, Eisenhoffer, Opata, Híres-Hirzer, and Jeny—whereas the Egyptian strikers managed to score three times against the Hungarian defense. Half of that defense—Gyula Mándi-Mandl, Béla Guttmann II, and Obitz—was Jewish.

Experts have been trying to account for that defeat, one of the most baffling in the history of Hungarian soccer. The reasons given involve only Jewish players, but no attempt was made to use them as scapegoats because they were Jews. It was simply that the great majority of players on the team *were* Jews, so they naturally had a strong influence on the outcome of the match. György Molnár of the *MTK*, the best inside right of the period, had been injured and was unavailable. His replacement, the non-Jewish József Takács II, soon to become one of the greatest strikers, was also sidelined with injury. This necessitated the shifting of the heavily left-footed Eisenhoffer from his accustomed inside left position to the right, where his effectiveness was bound to suffer. Another dysfunction of portentous consequence was the inability of József Braun, the usually mobile and dangerous outside right, to shake himself loose from Salem, the tough-playing Egyptian left back. One of the designated penalty kickers, Braun also failed to convert a penalty in the first half, an experience that was to haunt him for the rest of his otherwise brilliant career. Braun's frustration was shared by the rest of Hungary's Jewish strikers. Their sophisticated, technically well-prepared plays were repeatedly broken up by the tight Egyptian defense. The irony of it all is that Sweden, the eventual champion, had never won against Hungary. Had the Hungarian national eleven managed to hold out against Egypt, they might well have trounced Sweden and won the gold medal.

The success that eluded Hungary's Jewish Olympians in Paris was captured by four of them at the Olympic Games in Amsterdam in 1928. The sole gold medal for individual achievement was awarded to Dr. Ferenc Mező for his 100-page study, *The History of the Olympic Games,* which he had submitted for the epic works category of the artistic competition. The first Hungarian Olympic champion in 1928, whose presence in Amsterdam the Hungarian Olympic Committee had not considered essential, learned of the victory in Budapest. Indeed, except for a brief celebration, Mező, by his own recollection, was ignored through much of the quarter-century-long Horthy era simply because he was a Jew. He was a patriot and a scholar, having been wounded in the First World War and awarded high decorations. The first Olympic Games of modern times left an indelible impression on him; he was eleven years old in 1896. He subsequently became a teacher of Greco-Roman history and a lifelong student of the history of sports. He was a thorough researcher and a prolific and engaging writer. In addition to his gold-medal winning work, published in 1923, the result of twenty long years of labor, Mező was the author of forty-four books and numerous scholarly articles. He was also a tireless propagator of sports, giving countless lectures on a wide variety of related topics throughout Hungary.

After more than a decade and a half, Hungary recaptured the dominant role in fencing, sweeping both the individual and team saber competitions. For their contribution to the latter, three Jewish Olympians won gold medals: János Garay, the 1923 national champion; Sándor Gombos, who also placed fifth in the individual saber competition, and Attila Petschauer, one of Hungary's most gifted fencers.

According to the experts, the lion's share in Hungary's triumph in the team competition was Petschauer's. It came as a surprise to no one. Petschauer, who had won the Heroes' Memorial Tournament, the last of three pre-Olympic qualifying meets, and the title "the best Hungarian saber fencer," proved invincible. He overwhelmed his opponents by his unstoppable attacks, which were as flawless as they were extemporaneous, accompanied by his trademark shout, "Hollalah-oplah-allalah." In the course of the semifinals he won all of his twenty bouts. Petschauer's irrepressible humor and infectious optimism helped his teammates over-come anxiety and self-doubt, emotions that often grip athletes. Petschauer nearly repeated Fuchs's double Olympic victories in 1908 and 1912. How-ever, in the individual saber event he was defeated by Ödön Terstyánszky, his teammate and the eventual gold-medal winner, and finished second.

Another second-place finish, however, caused considerable disappoint-ment. Having won two consecutive European championships in 1926 and 1927, Hungary's national water polo team was the odds-on favorite to capture the gold medal. Anticipating victory, Béla Komjádi, the famous coach of the national team, made some key personnel changes, such as benching the experienced but aging Tibor Fazekas, one of the greatest Jewish players and a stalwart of the national team since 1920. Much to the astonishment of everyone, the Hungarians lost in the final to the Germans, whom they had beaten 8-1 in the European championship of 1927, by a score of 5-2. Defending the goal of the Hungarian national team was its only Jewish player, István Barta. He probably was the most disconsolate player in the water. Had he been able to save the shot which three seconds before the end of the game became the Germans' equalizing goal, the Hungarians would have climbed out of the pool as Olympic champions.

Among the wrestlers the newest link in the long line of Jewish champions demonstrated an impressive reservoir of skill, strength, and mobility. In the Greco-Roman featherweight competition the talented twenty-two-year-old Károly Kárpáti placed a respectable fourth. A virtual unknown, Kárpáti had finished second in the 1927 European championship.

The Great Depression cast an ominous light on preparations for the Tenth Olympic Games, scheduled to take place in Los Angeles in the summer of 1932. As late as 5 January 1932 the position of the government in Hungary was that it simply could not underwrite the expenses needed to send an Olympic team. Hungarian sport clubs were struggling on a mere subsistence level. Last-ditch efforts were made to raise the necessary funds. In a heart-rending letter signed by the chairman of the Hungarian Olympic Committee and a variety of sport, social, and commercial associations, a desperate appeal for financial support was made to Hungarians residing in the United States. Members of the Olympic swimming and water polo teams participated in exhibition tournaments in New York, Cleveland, Chicago, and San Francisco to raise funds. Prominent representatives of sports gave speeches throughout Hungary to rouse popular interest and solicit donations. On 21 April 1932 the Hungarian Olympic Society was formed. Its managing president and executive secretary was Alfréd Hajós-Guttmann, the two-time swimming champion of the 1896 Olympic Games, and Ferenc Mező, the 1928 winner of the gold medal in literature. Thanks to the success of their efforts and those of the Los Angeles Olympic Committee, which managed to come up with an economical package deal assuring reduced transportation for all participants to Los Angeles and room and board in the Olympic village, Hungary's Olympic team left for the New World for the second time.

No Hungarian-Jewish Olympian succeeded in winning a gold medal in individual competition. However, five Jews were among the members of Hungarian teams that battled their way to Olympic championships. Los Angeles's State Armory was the site of the team saber competition, in which Hungary trounced Denmark 15-1 and Mexico 14-2 in the preliminary rounds. The Hungarian team then went on to beat the United States 13-3, Poland 15-1, and Italy 9-2 in the finals. The Italians took the defeat so hard that they gave up the remaining bouts. The hero of the team competition was Endre Kabos, a quiet, unassuming twenty-six-year-old member of the European-champion Hungarian team (1931) and the second-place finisher in the 1931 European individual championship. He won fifteen of his sixteen bouts, more than any of his teammates. Kabos also finished third in the individual saber competition, behind György Piller, the gold medal winner and his teammate, and the Italian Giulio Gaudini, whom he defeated in the team competition. Attila Petschauer, the only other Jewish member of the Olympic champion Hungarian saber team, placed fifth in the individual competition.

The other Hungarian victory in team competition was as much the result of hard training and superb performance by a group of talented and determined players as the indefatigable labors of their much-loved and respected Jewish coach. Béla Komjádi, a legend in his time, was idolized by his players. A short, bald man of great simplicity who fended off lucrative contract offers from foreign teams with congenial aplomb, Komjádi regarded himself as the informing spirit of Hungarian water polo. His fanatical determination and enthusiasm, coupled with an unerring tactical clairvoyance and a brilliant, analytical knowledge of the intricacies of the game, lifted the Hungarian national team into the realm of the invincibles. Its performance in Los Angeles was an eloquent testimony to Komjádi's unwavering efficiency and soaring vision. It had three Jewish players. György Bródy, a regular, was a brilliant, elegant goalie who had a magnetic effect on the ball despite his peculiar habit of preferring to render even the most dangerous shots harmless by batting the ball down in front of him rather than catching or pushing it over the goalpost. Substitutes were Miklós Sárkány, a tough-playing, dependable and intelligent defensive back whose ability to block the angle of shots directed at the goal and to break up attacks by checking the forwards of opposing teams made him a virtual second goalie, and István Barta, an outstanding goalie who had been a member of Hungary's national team, the three-time winner of the European championship (1926, 1927, and 1931). Battling the unaccustomed effects of the California heat and the painful memories of the defeat in the 1928 Olympic final, the Hungarians played an inspired series of games, trouncing Germany 6-2, Japan 18-0, and the United States 7-0. The gold medal was the greatest and most timely gift they could have given their beloved coach. Komjádi, already ailing, basked only briefly in the glow of his "golden team." He died in March 1933, at the age of forty-one.

Two other Hungarian-Jewish Olympians won medals in Los Angeles. Károly Kárpáti, by then a three-time (1930-32) national champion, improved his earlier Olympic performance in the lightweight Greco-Roman wrestling. He finished second in the freestyle lightweight competition. In the individual saber competition Endre Kabos won the bronze. It was something of a disappointment for the hero of the team competition, for there he was in a better form than György Piller, the eventual gold-medal winner. Indeed, he defeated even the Italian Gaudini, who would win the silver medal. Petschauer placed fifth in the individual saber competition.

It retrospect, it seems astonishing that neither the promulgation in September 1935 of the Nuremberg Laws, which deprived the Jews living in Nazi Germany of citizenship and many civil rights, nor the prevailing atmosphere of chauvinism and militarism, should have failed to dissuade the members of the International Olympic Committee from bringing the Eleventh Olympic Games into Germany. Acknowledgement of the contributions which Jewish and "other racially inferior" athletes had made to the success of the modern Olympic Games and the Olympic reaffirmation of the basic principles of universal peace and the brotherhood of man should have been sufficient reasons for holding the Games elsewhere. However, the Nazis' promise to observe a modicum of civility and exercise restraint for the duration of the competition, in combination with the committee's all-too accommodating policy of remaining apolitical, assured a green light to proceed as planned. Amid jubilation and under Hitler's gaze the Olympic Games were opened in Berlin's giant Olympic Stadium on 1 August 1936.

Hungarian-Jewish Olympians scored a "solid gold" performance in the country whose official ideology institutionalized their racial inferiority. All of the medals they won were gold. The most important psychological victory was scored in the women's individual foil competition. For five days no Hungarian athlete won a medal or even placed behind the medal winners. On the sixth day the ice broke. Ilona Elek (Schacherer), a twenty-nine-year-old, two-time European champion, who played classical piano with as much virtuosity as she handled the foil (which she had grasped for the first time only eight years earlier), won Hungary's first gold medal in the 1936 Olympic Games. Her victory was a double slap in the Nazis' face. Not only was Elek half-Jewish, she also defeated Helen Mayer, her

German coreligionist, the gold-medal winner of 1928, whom the Nazis, at a considerable compromise of their racial ideology, had coaxed back from the United States. In two brilliantly fought cliffhangers she displayed a dazzling repertoire of lightning-quick moves as well as remarkable resiliency that enabled her to engineer repeated comebacks. "Csibi" Elek, in a nerve-wracking bout, edged Mayer 5-4 and defeated the Austrian Ellen Preis, the 1932 Olympic champion, 5-3. Even though she suffered an unexpected and painful setback at the hands of the German Hass, luck was on her side. Two former gold-medal winners battled and decided the outcome of the competition in favor of a third party. In a dramatic bout, Preis, who had already suffered two losses, handed Mayer her second defeat, leaving Elek with only one loss and the Olympic championship.

The second Olympic gold medal to be won by a Hungarian caused just as much consternation among the Nazis. The durable, tenacious Károly Kárpáti, competing in his third Olympic Games, was still going strong at age thirty. According to the experts only the favoritism the judges displayed toward Charles Pacombe, the world-famous French wrestler, had deprived Kárpáti of the gold medal in 1932. This time, however, neither the judges nor his opponents could stop him. In the enormous *Deutschlandhalle* the noise was deafening. Hitler, sitting among thousands of German wrestling fans, was treated to yet another humiliating spectacle. Ignoring the unsportsmanlike conduct of the spectators, who jeered every one of his moves while lustily applauding those of his opponents, Kárpáti defeated Wolfgang Ehrl, the powerful German national champion, in the final. It was his greatest and undoubtedly most satisfying victory.

The difficulty of establishing her Judaism persists in the case of Ibolya Csák, one of Hungary's preeminent athletes of the interwar period. The usually trustworthy Hungarian-Jewish grapevine shows three groups of disparate opinions. Some sources emphatically insist that she was Jewish, others cannot say for certain though will not rule out the possibility of it, and still others disagree firmly. I am including her here by reason of a convincing majority opinion.

Csák won Hungary's sole Olympic track-and-field medal at the 1936 Olympic Games. That distinction was surpassed only by the degree of surprise her accomplishment generated, even though she was by then a four-time national champion high jumper. She was eventually to win seven consecutive national titles (1933-39), a European championship, and two national titles in the broad jump. In 1936 Csák was already an athlete of Olympic championship quality. In 1930, when she was fifteen, she became a gymnast and later a sprinter. She first competed as a novice high jumper in March 1933. She progressed rapidly and won her first national title in 1935, by which time she was ranked fifth in the world. In the same year she married and seemingly turned her back on a promising athletic career. She spent much time keeping house and gardening. However, the twenty-year-old housewife, as she revealed subsequently, kept in a top physical shape by doing gymnastic exercises, chopping wood, and shoveling snow. Early in 1936 she returned to competition, and by the summer she jumped 161 centimeters, a new national record. In Berlin, however, in the absence of J. Shiley and M. Didrikson, the two American record holders, the German Ratjen was given the best chance to win the gold medal. However, only three jumpers—Csák, the sixteen-year-old Dorothy Odam of Great Britain, and Elfriede Kaun, the Germans' last hope—managed to clear 160 centimeters. In the course of the jump-off, the bar was raised by two centimeters. Twice all three failed to clear that height. In the last, nerve-wracking attempts both Odam and Kaun succumbed to the strains of the competition. But the national record Csák had set two months earlier was good reason to hope that the new height was within her reach. She was clearly in top form and apparently had not depleted the reservoir of her considerable talents. Calmly she made her last approach and jumped into the ranks of Olympic immortals.

Not since the victories of Jenő Fuchs in the 1908 and 1912 Olympic Games had the saber flashed as dangerously in the hand of a Jewish fencer as in Endre Kabos's. The only Jewish member of the Hungarian Olympic saber team was clearly the hero of the individual and team competitions. The tall, quietly witty twenty-six-year-old stalwart was by nature sensitive and brooding. Even though one of the best fencers in Hungary since the mid-1920s (interestingly he never won a national individual championship in the entire course of his brilliant career) Kabos, unlike the extroverted and optimistic Attila Petschauer, often felt out of place. He was discouraged by the multitude of anti-Semitic Hungarian army officers and fencing officials who made no secret of their dislike of Jews. They regarded even their Jewish teammates as unwelcome outsiders. It was not as if Kabos had not scored great successes in the early

1930s. He was a member of the 1930 national saber champion Tisza István Vívó Club, also placing third in the individual competition; he was on the 1932 Olympic saber champion team; and he won six gold medals and a silver in European championships between 1931 and 1935. Despite these victories, the frustrated Kabos had considered retiring from competition and even gave his saber away, after promises of flexible employment that would have allowed him to train and compete without financial worries had fallen through. He opened a grocery store, a time-consuming and physically demanding undertaking. At last, however, a benefactor offered him a more suitable position, making it possible for Kabos to resume training. He stormed back into the limelight in time to be selected for the 1936 Hungarian Olympic team. If anti-Semitism in Hungary had caused him to feel uneasy and dispirited, how would he bear up under the pressure of competition in the shadow of the swastika-bearing flags that draped the capital of Nazi Germany? To the delight of his teammates and the discomfiture of his opponents, Kabos came through apparently unscathed by the discouraging memories of the past and unaffected by the Nazi paraphernalia. His concentration and patience enabled him to utilize favorable opportunities with dynamic outbursts, alternating defensive and offensive postures with dazzling speed and unerring efficiency.

In the final rounds of the team saber competition the Hungarians clashed with the Olympians of Nazi Germany and Fascist Italy. They trounced the former 13-3. Against Italy, the customary cliff-hanger took place. With Italy leading 4-3 Kabos and Gustavo Marzi, the best Italian, stepped on the piste. Marzi, displaying a nearly flawless form, was leading 4-1 when Kabos stormed back. In a series of inspired counterattacks Kabos wiped out Marzi's lead and amid the cacophonous cheers of the crowd lunged for the last touché, defeating the Italian 5-4. Most experts agree that the outcome of the Kabos-Marzi bout turned things around for the Hungarians. They went ahead to defeat the Italians 9-6 and won the championship.

Kabos's second gold medal was as much the result of his exceptional fencing ability as a gift of the unpredictably shifting course of the final round robin. The Italian Marzi, in a graceful act of revenge, defeated Kabos 5-2 but was in turn edged by another Hungarian, Aladár Gerevich, and later trounced—unexpectedly—by the Polish Sobik. Another potential medal winner, the Italian Vincenzo Pinton, had no luck against either Hungarian. Thus Kabos, with only one loss, became Olympic champion.

It was a poignant yet disturbing picture, the strange blending of dissonant themes, clashing images, and implacable enemies in the surging emotions of the Olympic drama. A Hungarian Jew stood at attention as the anthem of his Fascist nation was played, engulfed by thousands of German spectators with their arms raised in the Nazi salute. The world's greatest saber fencer savored the most precious moments of his brilliant career. The memory of it would last a lifetime, but that lifetime was to last only a little more than eight years. On 4 November 1944 Endre Kabos was one of the many people who fell to their deaths in the cold, dirty waters of the Danube from a bridge which the Nazis and their Hungarian Arrow Cross lackeys had mined and prematurely exploded.

The unforgettable legacy of a Jewish coach and two Jewish players helped Hungary retain Olympic preeminence in water polo. Béla Komjádi's love and knowledge of the game left an indelible imprint on the style and technique of the Hungarian national water polo team; György Bródy, the brilliant goal-defying goalie was playing for his second Olympic title; and Miklós Sárkány was the powerful defensive player who had since the 1932 Olympics become a regular member of the team. The Hungarians romped through the early rounds without a single loss (Yugoslavia, 4-1; Malta, 12-0, Great Britain, 10-1; Belgium, 3-0; Holland, 8-1). On a rainy and chilly 14 August they battled the Germans to a 2-2 tie in the *Schwimmstadium,* where 20,000 German fans shouted deafening encouragement. Thus the decisive matches were played the following day. Germany beat Belgium 4-1. Hungary had to win by a wider margin of goals against France to retain its better goal average and the Olympic title. In a nerve-wracking match of many missed opportunities on both sides, Bródy proved unbeatable. He shut out the French offensive line, while the quickly executing Hungarian attackers five times succeeded in rendering the French goalkeeper helpless. Few Hungarians failed to bring to mind Uncle Komi—as Komjádi was respectfully called—on that tearfully joyous day. The late "Great Master" earned Hungary's second consecutive gold medal in water polo as much as did the players he had coached to world fame.

The Olympic fire that burned so courageously in the oppressive air of Nazi Germany soon began to flicker and finally was extinguished by forces that set out to prove their superiority not by competition but by destruction. Three years after the close of the 1936 Olympic Games human life became a matter of no consequence and the obsessive pursuit of a martial and racial dream of making *Deutschland über alles* a reality swept away the fragile house of cards. For the second time in a quarter of a century the lights were going out.

Though the preparation for and participation in the Olympic Games were a major part of Hungarian sport activity, there were also significant achievements in the extra-Olympic realms of sport. In Hungary as elsewhere, the true depth and diversity of Jewish participation in sports was more easily discernible in the broad national spectrum than within the restrictions imposed by the Olympic rules. Because of stringent limitations, the number of athletes selected every four years revealed but the tip of the iceberg. Furthermore, Olympic success or failure depended on a single day's all-or-nothing performance, where "best" is fleeting and subject to many variables. By contrast, participation in national competition provided for a more consistent and extended exposure.

One of the fastest and most durable sprinters of the 1920s was Ferenc Gerő, who won national titles in the 100 meters (1921-24 and 1928) and 200 meters (1922-24). He was a member of the 4 x 100-meter relay national champion Kereskedelmi Alkalmazottak Országos Sport Egyesülete (1921-25 and 1928), a team that featured other outstanding Jewish sprinters such as Béla Helfer, Antal Vogel, Béla Vida, Mór Gerő, István Steinmetz, and István Sugár. In the 1930s Gábor Gerő of the *MTK* won national championships in the 100 meters (1932) and the 200 meters (1931 and 1933). In the middle and long distances István Grosz of the *MTK* won an impressive number of national titles (800 meters, 1918; 1500 meters, 1920; 5000 meters, 1924-26).

In contrast to the growing number of Jewish male athletes there appeared to be no comparable interest among women in any of the events of the broad spectrum of track and field. The sole exception was Györgyi Widder of the *BEAC,* who sprinted to a national title in the 100 meters in 1932.

Though they left no lasting impression in European, world or Olympic competition, the following Jewish boxers fought their way into the select company of national titleholders: Zsigmond Ádler (flyweight, 1925), Miklós Gelb (bantamweight, 1925; featherweight, 1937-40); Imre

Mándi-Mandl (lightweight, 1939; welterweight, 1935, 1937-38); Béla Baron (middleweight, 1939); József Frank (light heavyweight, 1923; heavyweight, 1926); Gyula Grosz (heavyweight, 1927). In addition to winning individual national titles, Jewish boxers such as Miksa Hochmann and Ödön Krausz (Terézvárosi Torna Klub, 1926-27) and József Askenázi (Budapesti Testgyakorlók Köre, 1936) were members of teams that won national championships.

Unlike their coreligionists in boxing, Jewish chess players won international fame. Endre Steiner was a member of the Hungarian team that won three world championships (1927-28 and 1936) and twice (1930 and 1937) placed second; Lajos Steiner played for the 1936 world champion team; and Andor Lilienthal was a member of the national team that placed second in the 1937 world championship in Stockholm.

Interestingly, the strong showing of Hungarian-Jewish fencers in the interwar Olympic Games was not the direct result of a multitude of Jewish fencers coalescing in the course of national competitions. In fact, except for the world-famous Jewish Olympians, the paucity of outstanding Jewish fencers in the interwar period was nothing short of astounding. Only two Jews, both Olympians, won national championships in the men's saber individual competition: János Garay in 1923 and Sándor Gombos in 1930. Both were also members of teams that won national team titles in the 1920s. However, neither Attila Petschauer nor Endre Kabos, the heroes of the 1932 and 1936 Olympic team and individual championships respectively, ever won a national individual title. Kabos was a member of the 1930 national saber team champion, the Tisza István Vívó Club and of the Újpesti Torna Egylet. In 1937 he helped the latter break the monopoly of the army officers' Honvéd Vívó Klub, which had held the national épée team title since 1931, and remain national champion for two more consecutive years. Petschauer won his only national title in the saber team competition in 1929 as a member of the Nemzeti Vívó Club.

A similar lack of depth was the most surprising feature of the achievements of Jewish women in fencing. Despite her remarkable victory in the Berlin Olympics, Ilona Elek by no means dominated the women's foil individual national championships. In fact, 1936 was the climacteric of the interwar phase of her career, when, in addition to the Olympic championship, she also won the national title. She, however, failed to retain it in the following year. It may have been of consolation to her that the

1937 national champion was Margit Elek, her younger sister, who was also a member of the Detektive Atlétikai Klub, the team that won the 1938 national title. The two Eleks were a more dominant force in international fencing. Ilona was a member of Hungary's world champion foil team in 1937 and finished second in the individual competition; she was European champion in 1934 and 1935 and helped the Hungarian team to three consecutive European titles (1933-35) and a second place (1936). Margit followed closely in her sister's footsteps, duplicating her record in team competition. It was in the individual competition that she was overshadowed by her sister. Margit finished second to Ilona in the 1934 European championship and placed fourth in 1935. The Elek sisters, however, shared more than talent, achievement and fame. Their remarkable durability would allow them to overcome the psychological scars of discrimination and the adverse physical effects of being forcibly sidelined between 1940 and 1945 and to resume their careers with renewed vigor and unwavering determination. Athletes in their thirties and forties rarely compete in world-class tournaments, let alone dominate them. Yet, between 1946 and 1956 the Eleks would amass an astounding number of Olympic, world, European, and national titles, becoming the most successful women fencers in the history of the sport.

Between 1926 and 1934 soccer in Hungary was a fully professional sport, pressed into the service of business interests. The number of outstanding Jewish players, though not as many as in the preceding period, was still impressive. The consensus was that four of them belonged on the "golden team" of those years. Ferenc Híres-Hirzer was a holdover from the "golden team" of 1919-26. The three new outstanding Jewish players were János Aknai-Acht, Gyula Mándi-Mandl, and Márton Bukovi.

A tall, well-built player noted for his speed and lightning-quick reflexes, Aknai-Acht was one of the truly memorable goalkeepers in the history of Hungarian soccer. Those who watched him play in the late 1920s and early 1930s recall with awe the acrobatic moves with which he guarded the goal of the *UTE*. He was tapped for the national team ten times. He could have been the best in his position, but unfortunately for all his brilliantly executed feats, he could also make mistakes that would have been unbecoming even in a novice. No goalkeeper can afford the luxury of oscillating between such extremes. Had he been able to improve his reliability he would have remained an outstanding goalkeeper for the rest of the interwar years.

No such imperfections flawed the style of Gyula Mándi-Mandl. Most defensive players up to his time were powerfully built, using body checks effectively and sending the ball forward with huge, liberating kicks. Mándi-Mandl, on the other hand, was of slight build, almost fragile, and on first sight generated no confidence. No one seems to recall if he ever kicked the ball—or if he in fact could—with force or to any great distance. However, what he lacked in size and strength he compensated for with great intelligence, an uncanny ability to position himself disruptively and find the most effective—usually unspectacular—defensive solution against all types of attack. He handled the ball more like a midfielder, executing only short kicks and passes. His unorthodox style eventually found a growing number of admirers and imitators. The "virtuoso of positioning and the world champion of timing," as he was reverently called by his contemporaries, was also a remarkably resilient and durable player. In 1924, at the peak of his career, Mándi-Mandl, then twenty-five, suffered a severe knee injury. For five years he grappled with the psychological and physical problems of recovery. He not only returned to active play but regained his form as well. He was nearly forty when he retired, leaving an indelible imprint on future generations of Hungarian defenders. Between 1921 and 1934 Mándi-Mandl was selected thirty-one times for Hungary's national eleven.

Like a general with the capacity to inspire by example and leadership, Márton Bukovi, playing in his pivotal position of center halfback, directed the defense of the *FTC,* the team on which he played for seven years (1926-33). He was a strong player of consummate skill both in the air and on the ground. His moves were unpredictable. He could play with the authority of a tough defender or the quick intelligence of a playmaker. His style was unspectacularly efficient yet immensely crowd-pleasing. Following the recovery from an injury, Bukovi left for France, where he played with great success for years. Like Mándi-Mandl, he would become one of Hungary's most respected coaches after the Second World War. He represented Hungary eleven times in international matches.

By the middle of the 1930s the seemingly unending flow of outstanding Jewish players had been reduced to a trickle. The professional experience proved short-lived. Some players left Hungary in response to lucrative offers, others retired. For the first time since the introduction of soccer into Hungary there was no new generation of Jewish players. In the "golden team" of 1935-38 László Sternberg and Ferenc Sas-Sohn were the only Jewish players, and also the last ones to be selected for a "golden team." Two more suitable players could hardly be found. Sternberg was a nonpareil defender. His flawless technique and calm, intelligent style meshed well with the great speed and firm, always sportsmanlike authority with which he broke up attacks or tackled. He was particularly effective in using the sliding tackle. He is also vividly remembered for his ability to control the ball with either foot, an asset respected and envied by most soccer players. He played for the Újpest Futball Club, helping it to win two first-division titles (1932-33 and 1934-35). He played nineteen times on Hungary's national team between 1928 and 1936.

Ferenc Sas-Sohn of the Hungária Futball Club was the last of the great Jewish right wingers. A small, rather timid player who preferred to avoid clashes with the defense of the opposing teams, Sas-Sohn distinguished himself with his speed, dribbling ability, and accurate passes. Between 1936 and 1938 he played for Hungary seventeen times and scored two goals. His best performance it is recalled, was in an otherwise unmemorable match against Ireland (3-3 on 3 May 1936). Though he scored none himself, all three Hungarian goals came through his efforts. He passed to György Sárosi I, the legendary sixty-one-time international center, for the first goal. A desperate Irish defender batted away Sas-Sohn's deceptively arched pass by hand. Again Sárosi scored from the resultant penalty. Hungary gained the equalizer when Sas-Sohn's powerful shot deflected from a defender into the Irish goal. International recognition capped the high-water mark of his career. In 1937 the twenty-two-year-old Sas-Sohn was selected for a team representing Central Europe in a match against the best of Western Europe. Playing in the Olympic Stadium in Amsterdam, the Central Europeans won 3-1, two of their goals having been scored by the Hungarian-Jewish winger.

Sas-Sohn also had the sad distinction of being the last Jewish player to be selected for an interwar Hungarian national team. Following Hungary's disheartening 2-4 loss to Italy in the final of the 1938 World Cup in Paris, he left Hungary and settled in Argentina. His departure disappointed legions of soccer fans, but for him the passage of the First Jewish Law (May 1938) was a clear sign of doom which few Hungarian Jews were willing or able to recognize.

Though not regarded as one of the all-time best of the best, fans of the *FTC* still fondly recall the left winger whose speed and dynamism made him an invaluable member of the offense. In the course of his six-year career (1933-39), all of which he spent with the *FTC,* Tibor Kemény played 202 first division matches and scored a hundred goals. His was the classic style of the winger: a quick sprint by the sideline ending in the accurate centering of the ball or a powerful shot at the goal. Despite his limitations—he was exclusively left-footed and ineffective in the air— Kemény established a respectable reputation that earned him nine international caps. He was only twenty-six when he retired, his career cut short by the passage of the law that barred all Jews from sport clubs and athletic competition.

After Hajós-Guttmann's remarkable double victory in the 1896 Olympic games, Jewish swimmers seemed to take a long leave of absence from international fame. The interwar years produced outstanding Jewish swimmers who won a respectable number of national titles. However, only one, Ödön Gróf of the *UTE,* may be regarded as having been a world-class competitor. In 1934 he was a member of the Hungarian 4 x 200-meter freestyle relay team that won a European championship in Magdeburg and finished second in the 1936 Olympic Games. In national competition Gróf proved to be extraordinarily versatile and successful. Except for the 100-meter freestyle, he dominated all distances in the latter half of the 1930s. His national titles—200 meters, 1937-38; 400 meters, 1935-39; 800 meters, 1936-39; 1500 meters, 1936-38; river swimming, 1940; 4 x 100-meter (1937-38, 1940-41, 1943) and 4 x 200-meter (1938, 1940-41) freestyle relay, however impressive, were only partially indicative of his talent and durability. The twenty-five-year-old Gróf might well have been able to add to the string of his national titles had Hungary's sweeping anti-Jewish laws not put an end to his brilliant career.

The achievements of Jewish swimmers in the 100- and 200-meter breaststroke distances were also impressive, though not in international competition. In 1928 László Köves-Steiner of the *MTK* won the 100-meter national championship. In the late 1930s, matching Gróf's prodigious success, György Angyal-Engel of the *UTE* was the dominant force, winning consecutive national titles (100 meters, 1937-40; 200 meters, 1938-39). He was also an excellent freestyle swimmer, a member of the *UTE*'s

4 x 100-meter (1940) and 4 x 200-meter (1938) national champion relay teams. His career, like Gróf's, came to a halt when the authorities decided to make sport in Hungary *Judenfrei.*

Swimming was also one of the three sports in which Jewish women excelled (fencing and table tennis were the others). In the interwar years their performance was limited to national competition. They were, however, pacesetters, establishing a tradition that was the lead to remarkable achievements in international competition in the wake of the Holocaust. National champions were Irén Dénes (100-meter freestyle, 1923-24), Ella Molnár (100-meter breaststroke, 1924-26), Katalin Kraszner (100-meter breaststroke, 1923-24; all-round swimming, 1924), Vilma Kraszner (member of the 3 x 100-meter medley team of the *MUE,* 1926-27, and 4 x 100-meter backstroke relay team of the *UTE,* 1930), Katalin Szőke (100-meter backstroke, 1926-29, and member of the 3 x 100-meter medley team of the *MUE,* 1926-27), and Magda Felhős (200-meter individual medley, 1940).

Notable Jewish achievements were also evidenced in diving. The first to win a national diving title was József Szalai, an outstanding gymnast of the *VAC,* who finished first in the springboard competition in 1922. It was his only national diving title. László Vajda left a more lasting impression as Hungary's preeminent diver of the 1920s and 1930s. He was a four-time (1924-25, 1927-28) national springboard champion and won the national highboard title five times (1929-30, 1933-35).

Notwithstanding the great interest it attracted among the socially prominent segments of Hungarian Jewry, tennis, unlike most other sports, failed to generate a commensurate competitive spirit. It was also the only sport in which the achievements of Jewish women outweighed those of Jewish men. No Jewish player ever won a national title in the men's singles. The best showing by a Jewish player belonged to Kálmán Aschner, a member of a wealthy family of industrialists that had long been associated with the *UTE,* one of the most famous Hungarian sport clubs. In 1938 Aschner, playing with a non-Jewish partner, Ottó Szigeti, by then a two-time singles national champion, won the national doubles title. His brother, Pál, teamed up with Magda Baumgarten to win a national title in the mixed doubles in 1930. The two Aschners were also members of the *UTE*'s 1933 and 1934 national champion team.

The performance of Jewish women in competitive tennis left a firmer impression both in quality and quantity. In addition to the mixed doubles title, her first triumph in a national championship, Magda Baumgarten won the women's singles and doubles national titles in 1931 and was a member of the 1934 national team champion *UTE,* which included another Jewish player, Lili Korein. In 1935 Lili Sárkány and in 1940 Zsuzsa Körmöczy, destined to become Hungary's greatest player, won national doubles titles. In 1940 Körmöczy also won in the national mixed doubles championship, playing alongside the non-Jewish József Asbóth, by then a two-time national singles champion. Sárkány and Körmöczy played for the *BBTE,* helping it to win a national team championship in 1940. The Jewish Laws ended Sárkány's career, and kept the talented sixteen-year-old Körmöczy out of competition for nearly five years.

The legacy of the fabled Richárd Weisz in weightlifting was nurtured by only a few powerful men. Andor Grünfeld was the lone Jewish weightlifter to win an individual national title. He was the featherweight champion of Hungary in 1936. In the team competition the Schweitzer brothers, Mihály and Oszkár, were members of the *UTE*'s 1936 national champion team. Weisz's successors in wrestling fared considerably better. In Greco-Roman wrestling Armand Magyar (bantamweight, 1924-27), József Pongrácz-Pollák (featherweight, 1920), Ödön Radvány (featherweight, 1924), Károly Kárpáti (featherweight, 1928; lightweight, 1930-32), Imre Surányi-Sturm (welterweight, 1930), and Tibor Fischer (heavyweight, 1920) won national titles. However, there was an inexplicable paucity of Jewish national champions in freestyle wrestling. Only Jenő Fehér-Weisz (featherweight, 1931) and the ubiquitous and durable Károly Kárpáti (lightweight, 1931) lit up an otherwise bleak record of achievements.

The imbalance in figure skating was even more pronounced. No outstanding Jewish athlete emerged in the interwar period to carry on the tradition in individual competition. However, in the late 1920s pairs figure skating became popular, both socially and competitively, in Hungary. The top pair consisted of Emilia Rotter and László Szollás. Like Ibolya Csák's, their religious origin is a matter of dispute. Some individuals in Hungary who profess knowledge about the social and religious background of figure skaters in the interwar period are of the opinion that neither was Jewish. There exists, however, a convincing piece of evidence that leads to a contrary conclusion. It is an apparently forgotten matter of record that Rotter and Szollás accepted an invitation to compete in the Second Winter Maccabiah Games, in which only Jewish athletes participated. It was held in 1935, at the height of their career,

at Banska Bistrica, Czechoslovakia. Official pressure exerted by Hungarian sports authorities, due to the persistently hostile relations between
the governments of Hungary and Czechoslovakia, caused Rotter and
Szollás to bow out. By then their reputation in national and international competition had been firmly established.

It is interesting to note that success abroad preceded Rotter and Szollás's first victory in a national championship on the ice of Budapest's
picturesque Városliget. In 1930 and 1931 they finished second in European championships. They captured the first of their six consecutive
national titles in 1931, the year in which they also became world champions. The following year they finished second. They recaptured the world
title in 1933 and held it for two more years. The pinnacle of their career
was in 1934, when they simultaneously held the national, European, and
world titles. Their Olympic performance was only slightly less spectacular,
bronze medals in 1932 and 1936. Rotter and Szollás were pacesetters,
but destined to be the last act. No Jewish figure-skating pair would glide
after them.

In no sport does the achievement of Jewish players justify the use of
more superlatives than table tennis. Indeed one is hard-put to account
for the number and magnitude of victories in this sport. Three partial
explanations come to mind: the great popularity of table tennis in Budapest in the early 1920s; the devotion and unrelentingly hard training
methods of players, despite the absence of qualified coaches and ready
availability of funds for equipment and travel; and the introduction of
the rubber-covered paddles, which revolutionized the game by replacing
the prevailing unimaginative slow, basically defensive pushing of the ball
with a highly mobile, quick-paced, and uninhibited style, the most prominent features of which were the powerful and accurate backhand and
the defensive chop and spin. Still, for the spectacle of fifty world championship titles which Hungarian men and women won before the outbreak
of the Second World War the clues lead nowhere. Neither can the surviving
Jewish players of that period shed light on the causes of that remarkable
string of victories. There seem to be no discernible circumstances or events
that would convincingly explain why table tennis even became a Hungarian monopoly, let alone a Jewish sport.

And a Jewish sport it was. The tidal wave began to surge in 1925 and
only the elimination of Jews from sports forced it to subside a decade and
a half later. In the men's singles, Jewish national champions succeeded

one another as naturally as if it were a birthright. Zoltán Mechlovits, a prewar national champion (1911), demonstrated his durability by winning two more national titles (1925-26) at the age of thirty-four. Sándor Glancz interrupted Mechlovits's winning streak by capturing the title in 1927. In the following year Mechlovits again proved invincible. Between 1929 and 1932 Miklós Szabados and Viktor Barna alternated as national champions. Their grip on the national title was loosened by Lajos Dávid in 1933, but Szabados stormed back in 1934. The next three champions, Tibor Házi (1935), Károly Benkő II (1936), and György Gárdos II (1937), were non-repeaters. In 1938 six years after his last triumph, Barna won his third individual national title. The last two Jewish national champions were Jenő Schmiedl (1939) and Tibor Barna III (1940), Viktor's brother.

The men's doubles displayed much the same Jewish prowess, though with less diversity. The durable Mechlovits repeated his standout performance, winning the second of his two national doubles titles alongside the non-Jewish Roland Jacobi. (One of the best Hungarian players of the time, Jacobi is often mistakenly identified as a Jew because of his "Jewish-sounding" family name.) Fourteen years later, in 1925, Mechlovits teamed up with Dániel Pécsi, of the *MTK,* and the Austrian Erwin Freudenheim and won the title in two consecutive national championships (1925-26). However, Mechlovits failed to win three in a row. Again the spoiler was Sándor Glancz. He and László Bellák, his teammate in the predominantly Jewish Nemzeti Sport Club, became national doubles champions in 1927. Mechlovits staged a spectacular comeback in the following year. Ably assisted by Dániel Pécsi, he regained the doubles title.

A new era dawned in 1929. Miklós Szabados and Viktor Barna, both of the *MTK,* won their first national doubles championship, which they retained three more consecutive times, relinquishing it in 1933 to two of their teammates and coreligionists, István Boros and Béla Nyitrai. The next three years were again dominated by Szabados, winning with Tibor Házi in 1934 and 1935 and with László Bellák in 1936. For two more years the domination of all-Jewish pairs continued. Károly Benkő II and Jenő Schmiedl won in 1937 and Barna, teaming up with István Boros, won his fifth national doubles title in the following year.

The year the Second World War broke out marked the beginning of the end of the Jewish monopoly of the national doubles title. Jenö Schmiedl was the harbinger of the inevitable transition. The last of the great Jewish doubles players, Schmiedl teamed up with non-Jewish partners—

Ferenc Soós in 1939-1940 and József Farkas in 1941—and won three national titles. He brought to a close the most remarkable series of victories by Jewish players in the history of table tennis.

In the women's singles, quantity fell short of quality. Only two Jewish players won national singles titles. Mária Kornfeld (1925) and Anna Sipos (1926-27, 1931, 1935, and 1939). Sipos was also an outstanding doubles player. She won the national title between 1929 and 1933, in 1935 and 1939-40, though never with a Jewish partner. Dóra Beregi was another prominent doubles player, a national champion in 1937 and 1938.

The record of Jewish achievements in mixed doubles was again impressive both in quality and quantity. Between 1926 and 1939 only two of the female halves of the teams that won national championships were non-Jews. The list of the winning teams is yet another reminder that table tennis was indeed a Jewish sport: 1926, Zoltán Mechlovits and Lili Friedmann; 1927, László Bellák and Anna Sipos; 1928, Mechlovits and Mária Mednyánszky (non-Jewish); 1934, Szabados and Mednyánszky; 1935, Szabados and Sipos; 1936, Bellák and Ida Ferenczy (non-Jewish); 1937, Ernő Földi and Dóra Beregi; 1938, Barna and Beregi; 1939, Jenő Schmiedl and Anna Sipos.

If the Jewish champions in the singles and doubles competition revealed but the tip of the iceberg, competition in the men's and women's team titles exposed the rest: the full extent of Jewish contributions to table tennis in Hungary. It enabled many excellent Jewish players to savor brief moments of glory and limelight in which the well-known singles and doubles champions basked. Between 1926 and 1941 the majority of the players on the national champion men's teams, such as the Magyar Testgyakorlók Köre, Nemzeti Sport Club, Budapest Sport Egyesület, Duna Sport Club, and Újpesti Sport Egylet, were Jewish. The 1939 national champion *VAC* was of course exclusively Jewish. There were fewer Jewish players on national champion teams in the women's competition. Two of the three players of the *MTK*—Lili Friedmann and Ilona Zádor—were Jewish. The *MTK,* winning four consecutive national titles (1937-40), shared the title in 1940 with the all-Jewish *VAC,* whose players went on to win the national team title in 1941. That was the last major collective victory by Jewish table tennis players in wartime Hungary.

World championships, especially in non-Olympic sports, are usually regarded as the supreme test of skill, courage, perseverence and imagination. Between 1926 and 1937 the Hungarians turned virtually all categories of world championships into a replay of their national championships. Except in 1926, when Roland Jacobi ruled the tables, and in the women's competition, where for years Mária Mednyánszky had no equals, Jewish players dominated the events. And except for 1926, the year the first world championship in table tennis was held in London, when the Hungarian team consisted of two Jewish players and two non-Jewish ones, and for Jacobi's last appearance in 1928, only Jewish players represented Hungary in the next eight world championships, winning seven titles and once placing second in the team competition. Victories in the singles and doubles competition were assured with a similar monotony.

The following statistics provide ample evidence of the astounding achievements of Hungary's Jewish world champions.

Viktor Barna: 22 gold medals (1929, doubles and team; 1930, singles, doubles and team; 1931, doubles and team; 1932, singles, doubles, and team; 1933a (Baden bei Wien), singles, doubles, and team; 1933b (Paris), singles, doubles, and team; 1935, singles, doubles, mixed doubles, and team; 1938, team; 1939, doubles), six silver medals (1931, singles; 1938, doubles; 1931, 1933b, mixed doubles; 1932, 1937, team), and three bronze medals (1938, singles; 1933a, doubles; 1930, mixed doubles).

Miklós Szabados: 15 gold medals (1931, singles; 1929, 1930, 1931, 1932, 1933b, 1935, doubles; 1930, 1931, 1933b, mixed doubles; 1929, 1930, 1931, 1933b, 1935, team), six silver medals (1929, 1932, 1935, singles; 1932, mixed doubles; 1932, 1937, team), and two bronze medals (1933b, singles; 1935, mixed doubles).

Anna Sipos: eleven gold medals (1932, 1933a, singles; 1930, 1931, 1932, 1933a and b, 1935, doubles; 1929, 1932, 1935, mixed doubles), six silver medals (1930, singles; 1930, 1931, 1933b, mixed doubles; 1933b, 1935, team), and four bronze medals (1929, 1931, singles; 1929, doubles; 1933a, mixed doubles).

László Bellák: seven gold medals (1938, mixed doubles; 1928, 1930, 1931, 1933b, 1935, and 1938, team), nine silver medals (1928, 1930, 1933b, singles; 1929, 1932, 1938, doubles; 1929, mixed doubles; 1932, 1937, team), and five bronze medals (1928, 1930, and 1935, doubles; 1931, 1933b, mixed doubles).

István Kelen: seven gold medals (1929, 1933b, mixed doubles; 1929, 1930, 1931, 1933b, 1935, team), five silver medals (1931, 1933a, doubles; 1930, 1936, mixed doubles; 1932, team), and two bronze medals (1930, singles; 1935, doubles).

Zoltán Mechlovits: six gold medals (1928, singles; 1926, 1928, mixed doubles; 1926, 1928, 1929, team), two silver medals (1926, singles; 1926, doubles), and three bronze medals (1929, singles; 1928, doubles; 1929, mixed doubles).

Sándor Glancz: four gold medals (1933a, doubles; 1928, 1929, 1933a, team), four silver medals (1929, 1932, 1933b, doubles; 1933a, mixed doubles) and six bronze medals (1933a, singles; 1928, 1930, doubles; 1930, 1931 and 1932, mixed doubles).

Lajos Dávid: four gold medals (1930, 1931, 1933a, 1933b, team), three silver medals (1931, 1933a, doubles; 1932, team), and one bronze medal (1930, singles).

Tibor Házi: three gold medals (1933b, 1935 and 1938, team), one silver medal (1933b, doubles), and four bronze medals (1933b, 1938, singles; 1932, 1936, doubles).

Dániel Pécsi: three gold medals (1926, doubles; 1926, 1928, team), and one silver medal (1928, mixed doubles).

István Boros: one gold medal (1933a, team), and three bronze medals (1932, singles; 1932, 1933a, doubles).

Ernő Földi: one gold medal (1938, team).

The last link to this remarkable chain of victories, unparalleled in the history of Jewish achievements in sports, was added by Viktor Barna. He teamed up with the Jewish, Austrian-born Richard Bergmann, the winner of the men's singles, to win the men's doubles title at the last prewar world championship (Cairo, 1939). For two more years Jewish players remained highly visible in national championships. By 1942 table tennis, falling in line with all other sports in Hungary, had become *Judenfrei*. The removal of Jewish players did not have devastatingly adverse effects. A new generation of non-Jewish players would represent Hungary creditably in most postwar world championships, a fact that attests to the depth of table tennis talent in that country. However, the puzzle of the fifteen-year-long dense concentration of outstanding Jewish players remains unsolved.

The Magyar and Magyarized family name of many a Jewish member of the Hungarian sport clubs could serve to conceal one's religious identity or at least keep it out of public display. No such option was available to the members of the *VAC* (Vívó és Atlétikai Club), the only exclusively Jewish sport club in Hungary. The uniqueness of *VAC* was an accurate reflection of the desire of the majority of Hungarian Jewry to uphold a well-delineated policy of assimilation. Despite the occasional manifestations of organized anti-Semitism, no plan of group defense through physical training was ever seriously entertained by the Jewish leadership. Consequently through most of its forty-year-long existence the *VAC* never was the athletic home for the majority of Hungary's sports-minded Jewish youth. Still, in the interwar period its membership increased considerably. It was also as patriotic as it was Hungarian. Under pressure from anti-Zionist communal leaders, the *VAC* bore little resemblance to the ideals of its founders and early members. The most convincing proof of the *VAC*'s outlook was that it conformed to the assimilationist and patriotic philosophy of the overwhelming majority of Jews engaged in competitive sports. As a result no Jewish male or female athlete ever represented Hungary in the World Maccabiah Games.

A review of the statistics of performance reveals that the *VAC*, on the whole, was not one of Hungary's top sport clubs. Yet it was by no means merely a gathering place of sports-minded Jewish youth hoping to engage in physical exercise in tranquility and safety. The members of the *VAC* regularly took part in national tournaments and championships. Wearing the insignia of the club, the badge of their Jewishness, was both a sign of athletic pride and an act of courage, for it was a virtual invitation to catcalls, sneering, and malicious remarks.

Though the *VAC* failed to attract more than a handful of Hungary's best Jewish athletes it left a creditable impression in a number of sports both in individual and team events. The *VAC*'s pride was József Szalai, one of Hungary's preeminent gymnasts in the 1920s and an outstanding diver. Another member, Tibor Landau, won a national championship on the horizontal bar in 1929. László Vajda, who dominated diving from the mid-1920s to the mid-1930s, won his first national championship in 1924 as a member of the *VAC.* He subsequently left the Jewish club for the *FTC,* where he remained for the rest of his brilliant career. In the mid-1930s István Sárkány brought honors to the *VAC* by winning national titles in gymnastics (parallel bars, 1934; horizontal bar, 1933). Károly Benkő II was a rarity among the Jewish table tennis players who dominated the sport, in that he was one of the two affiliated with the only Jewish sport club in Hungary. He was the 1936 national champion and won the 1937 national doubles title with his coreligionist Jenő Schmiedl of the *UTE.* The other was György Gárdos II, the winner of the 1937 national singles title. Both were members of the *VAC*'s 1939 national champion team. Of the *VAC*'s women players only Dóra Beregi attained national stature. One of the best doubles players of her time, Beregi was national women's doubles champion in 1937 and 1938 (she teamed up with non-Jewish players on both occasions) and won national mixed doubles championships in the same years, playing alongside two outstanding Jewish players, Ernő Földi and Viktor Barna. Yet it was the *VAC*'s women's table tennis team that pulled off one of the most astounding feats. Its obscure members—Mme Sándor Grünwald, Rózsi Singer, and Mme Béla Vermes—finished the 1940 season as cochampions with the powerful *MTK*, the holder of the national title since 1937, whose leading player, Mária Mednyánszky, was a world champion many times over. Their performance was not a one-time fluke. The scrappy *VAC* players went on to win the national women's team championship in 1941, the last time Jews were permitted to compete.

Two more achievements in team competition deserve to be remembered. In 1928, the first time a national championship was held in team handball the *VAC*'s men's team won the title. Another *VAC* team captured first place in 1934. Of the *VAC*'s players the following were selected to represent Hungary in international matches: István Andor-Auspitz (2 times, 1933-34), György Endrei-Engel (1 time, 1933), Imre Farkas-Freund (1 time, 1933), Andor Forrai-Frisch (3 times, 1933-35), Tibor Máté (7 times 1935-38), Endre Salgó (9 times, 1933-39), and István Serényi-Schlesinger (10 times, 1935-36).

Somewhat less auspicious was the *VAC*'s participation in soccer. Its team gained promotion into the first division in the 1921-22 season and finished a respectable sixth in a field of twelve. Its best showing, fifth place, came in the 1923-24 season. Subsequently, the *VAC*'s fortune progressively declined. In the following season it slipped to seventh place, finished tenth in 1925-26, and was relegated never to return to the first division. During those five seasons two of the *VAC*'s players were selected to represent Hungary in international matches. Lajos Fischer, a diminutive but fearless and quick-reflexed goalkeeper, was tapped nine times and Dezső Grosz II, a tough, speedy back of flawless technique, played twice among the national eleven. In 1926 both emigrated to the United States.

Jewish athletes who left Hungary in the interwar period were few. Those who left did so for personal reasons. Some sought their fortune abroad, dissatisfied with the meager rewards of amateur sports, others left to honor the lucrative professional contracts they had signed, playing for foreign teams. Still others ended their athletic careers altogether. However, the majority stayed. They shared the optimism of their patriotic and assimilated coreligionists who ignored the political danger signals of the interwar years and placed their unshakeable trust in the ambivalent political philosophy of Miklós Horthy. The regent of Hungary disliked Hitler as much as he did the Jews. However, he was a realist, recognized the Jews' utility, and kept the virulently anti-Semitic factions at bay. Prosperity and their notable and varied contributions to virtually all facets of Hungary's economic and cultural life created a sense of security, though it was false. The Jews were convinced that their investment in assimilationism and anti-Zionism had indeed paid handsome dividends. The winds of danger, they thought, would soon blow over. Such expectations were born of a mixture of illusion and self-deceit rather than a realistic appraisal of the political situation. It may also have been a last-ditch psychological stand, a desperate attempt to stave off rejection.

Except for the Zionists and some sharp-eyed observers of the ominous events in European politics who had consistently been warning of catastrophe, few Hungarian Jews were prepared to think realistically about the harbingers of the Holocaust. To acknowledge them would have been to admit that their faith in the continuation of the thousand-year-old coexistence of Jews and Hungarians, which Jewish leaders had traditionally regarded as mutually beneficial, was not well placed.

CHAPTER IV

ELITE COGS IN AN IDEOLOGIZED SPORT MACHINE

The German occupation and the subsequent rule of the Arrow Cross Party intimidated, humiliated, and largely annihilated an entire generation of athletes and their fans. The wearers of the yellow Star of David were forbidden to enter sport establishments, ousted from their clubs, and excluded from competition. The *MTK*, one of Hungary's oldest and most popular clubs, was dissolved and its facilities were transferred into the jurisdiction of the *MOVE*, an extreme right-wing sport organization.

No service in the national interest, including achievement in sport, provided shelter from the Nazi and Arrow Cross terror. The list of the martyrs of Hungarian sport, both those with left-wing political conviction and those who were Jewish, is a sad and sobering memento of the blind hatred, institutionalized persecution, and indiscriminate extermination to which only the occupation of Hungary by the Soviet Army brought a halt. The recollection of eyewitnesses sheds light on many an astonishing personal drama. Once the idols of millions, many Jewish athletes starved, were beaten, and died ignominious deaths.

The most frequently recounted—and probably the most hideous—was the fate of Attila Petschauer, one of Hungary's world-renowned fencers. The happy-go-lucky bohemian and eternal optimist struggled to retain a semblance of humanity and dignity amid deprivation and brutality in the labor service unit that took him to the Ukrainian town of Davidovka. He nearly succeeded. Staggering exhausted and starving on the street, the labor servicemen passed a group of Hungarian officers. Petschauer recognized one of them. It was Lt. Col. Kálmán Cseh, an equestrian, who, like Petschauer, participated in the Amsterdam Olympics of 1928. They were friends then. A godsend, Petschauer may have thought. "Kálmán," he whispered. The former Olympic teammate, however, turned to one of the officers. "Make things hot for the Jew!" Two days later fate caught up with Petschauer. He was ordered to undress in subzero weather, climb a tree and sing. He then was repeatedly beaten. The Russians liberated him but could not save him.

Not all Hungarian army officers were devoid of feelings of decency and compassion. When Endre Kabos, the Olympic fencing champion of 1936, was ordered to report to a labor service group in Vác, a certain Captain Konrád recognized him and arbitrarily discharged him. On 4 November 1944 a gas pipe exploded on Margit Bridge, one of the last links between Buda and Pest. Many people were killed. Kabos was crossing the bridge on an explosive-laden truck, which plunged into the icy waters of the Danube.

Other fencers who fell victim to the Nazis' relentless effort to make Hungary *Judenfrei* were János Garay, an Olympic and European champion, and Oszkár Gerde, a two-time Olympic champion. Both perished in Mauthausen.

Two of Hungary's most talented soccer players of the 1920s, everyone's favorite "Csibi" and "Pubi," József Braun and Henrik Nádler, shared the tragic fate of thousands of labor servicemen. Similarly, neither achievement nor fame would spare boxing greats Imre Mándi-Mandl and Béla Baron; swimming champions András Székely, Miklós Somogyi, and György Angyal-Engel; István Grosz, the outstanding middle- and long-distance runner, and Lajos Dávid, the three-time world champion (team) table tennis player. The eighty-five-year-old Ferenc Kemény, one of the founders of the modern Olympic movement, committed suicide along with his wife on 21 November 1944, in the midst of the raging Arrow Cross terror.

Alfréd Brüll, the legendary president of the *MTK* and one of the principal movers and patrons of Hungarian sports, was deported to Auschwitz. It is said that the notorious Doctor Mengele had a habit of reciting passages from Shakespeare as he directed the arriving Jews either to the left to be gassed or to the right to be assigned to hard labor. According to a survivor who happened to be standing next to the Hungarian sports leader, Brüll detected inaccuracies in Mengele's quotes and corrected them before he was motioned to the left.

After the last German and Arrow Cross troops were driven out by the advancing Soviet armies in April 1945, the political and economic power and social and cultural privileges of the ruling classes came to an end. But neither the precarious system of uneasy political coalition of the Social Democratic, Peasant, and Communist parties nor the redistribution of land and limited nationalization of industry that took place under the watchful eyes of Soviet occupation forces managed to provide the war-torn country the means of recovery, stabilization, and progress. The coalition government was unable to extricate itself from a ever-deepening quagmire of intrigue and dissent. The new economic policy was rendered ineffective by deflationary monetary measures, increasing deficits, and unregulated market prices and wages. During the winter of 1947-48 the Communists seized power and put an end to coalition politics. A government of uncompromising Stalinists took charge.

As long as state intervention in society and the economy was limited and uneven, Hungary's much-suffering Jewry showed signs of renewed vitality. Many synagogues were rebuilt and became centers of religious and cultural rebirth. Increasing opportunities in private enterprise resulted in an enthusiastic response from Jewish merchants and lesser industrialists. Zionist organizations proliferated, and many Jewish youngsters looked to a revitalized *VAC* for athletic leadership.

The Communist takeover and the resulting changes that transformed the political, social, and economic structure had a crushing effect on the country's Jewry. Hungary became a carbon copy of the Soviet Union. Prime Minister and Communist Party First Secretary Mátyás Rákosi, a slavishly obedient Stalinist, became the guardian of the dictatorship of the proletariat. In the new atheistic society of working-class and peasant values the largely middle-class Jews became social outcasts and an economic liability. Despite the signing of an agreement on 7 December 1948 between the Jewish community and the government, guaranteeing religious freedom and safeguarding its full practice, to remain a professing Jew was a passport to nowhere. Jewish cultural life was purged of Israeli and Hebrew content, the Zionist organizations and the *VAC* were dissolved, and most Jewish high-school graduates were denied admission to universities because of their middle-class origin. Complete state control of the economy, leading to the indiscriminate nationalization of industry and the rejection of private enterprise, deprived Jews of their traditional means of livelihood yet offered little or nothing in return.

Despite the extensive damage the war had caused to sport facilities and the loss of some of the most outstanding athletes and sport leaders, sport in Hungary experienced a quick-paced reconstruction and produced enviable results. Within three years after the end of the fighting Hungary was well on its way to becoming a true superpower in the world of sports, a showcase of proletarian achievements.

Hungarian sport historians divide the postwar development of sport in Hungary into three phases. The revival of sport and physical education (from the end of 1944 to the beginning of 1948) was followed by the laying of socialist foundations (1948-63) which gave way to the unfolding of socialist sport (since 1963). It was made clear from the outset that the "comprehensive program of the Communist Party for the democratic transformation of the country" would reject the idea of keeping sport and ideology separate and subordinate the former to politics.

The biggest obstacle to proceeding beyond the purely objective description of the development of sport in postwar Hungary is the total absence of sources that approach it from a reliable perspective. That obstacle is, to be sure, not the result of the unwillingness or the inability of Hungarian sport historians to think and write objectively—elements of self-criticism do crop up in their works from time to time—but rather the constraints and limitations which the totalitarian state, especially in its initial stages of development, imposes on all sectors of society. That obstacle also hinders the identification of Jewish athletes, a task which is further complicated by the fact that neither the sport authorities nor the official organs of the Jewish community keep records of or make reference to the religious origin of sport figures. The former failed to do so as a matter of general policy; the latter because sport is one of the most jealously guarded state monopolies, in which no detraction, real or imagined, from socialist achievement was tolerated.

The quest for support of the masses at home and recognition abroad often created a need to circumvent the forbidding façade of the dictatorship of the proletariat. Such circumstances provided the means for the gradual reentry of Jewish athletes into the mainstream of Hungarian sports. Middle-class background was "forgiven" and religious origin became an unmentionable. Athletic training and achievement, like the work ethic of the nationalized industry and collectivized agrarian sector of the economy, served the national interest, not personal goals and aggrandizement. Preparations for national championships and international meets, but most of all for the approaching Olympic Games, demanded rigid discipline and unwavering commitment. Privileged status and the fringe benefits—well-paying jobs that provided generous amounts of time off for training and competition, guaranteed admission to universities, comfortable housing, favored treatment at customs upon return from foreign trips and the like—as well as the adulation of a sport-loving nation were inducements that few could or wanted to resist. In return, the authorities demanded total abandonment of the attitudes, values, and cultural preferences stemming from pre-Communist social position and schooling, or from the manifold influences of religious background. To all outward appearances that high price was paid. In some cases there were sustained inner conflicts and in one notable instance involving a 1952 Olympic swimming champion, Éva Székely, a public declaration of Jewish identity in 1974, long after her retirement from competition.

The effects of the Holocaust in Hungary left a shattered Jewish remnant which has managed to build a peculiar spiritual and cultural existence within the complicated constraints created by the uneasy toleration of the state. Notwithstanding the limits within which the Jewish community must operate if it is to survive at all, its synagogues, rabbis, theological seminary, cultural and charitable institutions have forged a standard of existence which Jewish communities in other socialist countries have long and vainly hoped for themselves. Still, because religious affiliation need not be registered, Jewishness manifests itself in two ways. To professing Jews it is a public declaration; to individuals who conceal their religious convictions and those who have abandoned it, it is a private matter. There is no documentary evidence to support the thesis that the profession of faith and the pursuit of athletic excellence may be mutually complementary. All that can be documented is religious background, not religious affiliation.

That as many Jews chose to stay in Hungary as did was surprising; that they should strive to make significant contributions in virtually all sectors of the emerging new society was astonishing. The traditions of immobility and assimilation provide only partial answers to this puzzling phenomenon. Memories of the unspeakable brutality of the Arrow Cross men, many of whom found integration into the socialist society easier than they had expected, and the experiences of ghetto life were still fresh when rumblings about Jews being overcompensated for their wartime losses and sufferings quickly spread, especially in the provinces. By the time anti-Jewish mob action in Kunmadaras, Miskolc, and Diósgyőr in the summer of 1946 was halted five Jews had been killed. The deep roots of popular anti-Semitism were undoubtedly strengthened by the widespread realization that the top Communist leaders—Mátyás Rákosi, Ernő Gerő, Mihály Farkas, and József Révai—were of Jewish origin. Though some Jews managed to leave the country before the Iron Curtain descended, the majority was trapped in virtual isolation.

The postwar achievements of Jewish athletes in Hungary adds yet another remarkable chapter to the annals of Jewish resilience and recovery. Of the surviving leaders Alfréd Hajós-Guttmann, Hungary's first —and first two-time—Olympic champion and Ferenc Mező, the noted sport historian and activist, became the architects of athletic reconstruction. The former was named president of the Hungarian Olympic Association in 1946; the latter was named to the International Olympic Committee in 1948.

The tragic wartime losses and the unfavorable political, social, and economic circumstances of the postwar era had short- and long-term negative effects. It is estimated that in 1946 the number of Jewish children under fifteen was only slightly over 15,000. Moreover, many Zionist youths left the country illegally within three years after the end of the war. It is against this forbidding backdrop that the record of Jewish achievement in sport would have to be understood and appreciated.

Hungary's interwar image as a superpower in table tennis had, with only a few notable exceptions, been built by Jewish men and women who dominated both national and international competition. Only one Jewish player managed to establish himself in world-class ranking in the postwar era: Péter Rózsás won national titles in the men's doubles (1966), singles (1967), and mixed doubles (1964, 1966-67) championships. He was European champion in the mixed doubles (1964) and men's doubles (1972). He was also a member of the three-time (1965-67) national team champion Budapesti Vasutas Sport Club. Between 1961 and 1968 Rózsás was selected for Hungary's national team ninety-two times.

Zsuzsa Fantusz was the sole heiress to the legacy of the outstanding Jewish women table tennis players of the interwar period. Though she failed to win a national singles, doubles, or mixed doubles title—a not unexpected result of her being a contemporary of the non-Jewish Gizella Farkas, perhaps the greatest player in the 1940s and 1950s—Fantusz experienced what it felt like to be among the best. She was a member of three national championship teams (*SZOT I,* 1951; *SZOT II,* 1953; Bp. Vasas Sport Klub, 1954-55). In the first half of the 1950s, the most successful period of her career, Fantusz six times represented Hungary in international competition. In world championship she was a two-time bronze medalist (1953 doubles and team) and placed fourth (1955 team). She won a gold medal (doubles) and placed fourth in the singles in the 1954 World University Games.

The achievements of György Fantusz, Zsuzsa's younger brother, were more modest and limited to the national scene. He played on the three-time (1957-59) national champion table tennis team of the Vasútépítő Törekvés Sport Klub.

In the area of track and field, Jewish participation plummeted to nothing. Although in the prewar era this was an event with a flourishing Jewish tradition, there is no sign that the tradition can be restored.

The spectacle of deterioration was only slightly less dramatic in soccer. In contrast to the unbroken continuity of generations of outstanding players in the pre-World War I and interwar periods, the post-1945 reconstruction of soccer was virtually devoid of Jewish participation. In addition, in the early 1950s there were as many active Jewish coaches as there were players. In fact, qualitatively the coaches—Gyula Mándi-Mandl, Márton Bukovi, and Béla Guttmann—were indubitably superior to the players. Of the three players who come into consideration only one compared favorably with the great predecessors. The career of Sándor Gellér, the goalkeeper of the *MTK*—or Textiles, Bp. Bástya, and Bp. Vörös Lobogó as the club was successively called to reflect, as other sport clubs did, the new socialist order—was adversely affected by being a contemporary of the non-Jewish Gyula Grosics, one of the world's greatest goalkeepers of the 1950s. Gellér is remembered for his dependability, tenacity, and diligence. He was twice member of a championship team (1951 and 1953) and although defended the goal of the national team only eight times between 1950 and 1956, he was Grosics's perennial substitute. Tamás Kertész, a right winger of the *FTC,* was a strong and fast player whose energetic attacking style—powerful shots and headers—and accurate passing caused many dangerous situations for the defense of opposing teams. He played 180 matches for his club between 1953 and 1960 and scored 54 goals. The high-water mark of his career came in October 1955, when he was twice chosen for the national team, then the most famous in the world, augmenting the legendary Kocsis-Tichy-Puskás-Czibor forward line. Both of his international matches ended in victory. The Hungarians beat Czechoslovakia 3-1 (October 2) and trounced Austria 6-1 (October 16). Kertész might have become a regular on the national team—a number of players alternated in the right winger's position, though none to the full satisfaction of the selector—had he not been prone to injury, an unfortunate liability that marred his entire career. A member of the *ETO* of Győr, Árpád Orbán was one of the few players from a provincial team to be tapped for the national eleven that represented Hungary in the Tokyo Olympics in 1964. His outstanding performance in the final against Czechoslovakia was instrumental in Hungary's 2-1 victory. However, it should be noted that neither Orbán's gold medal nor Hungary's Olympic performance in soccer may be considered a true measure of success. Orbán was the member of an Olympic team, but was not a member of the national eleven. As for Olympic soccer, the quality of the victory is tempered by the fact that since professional players are barred from the teams, and since in capitalist countries the best soccer is played by professionals, socialist countries tend to win the Olympic gold. Brazil, Uruguay, Italy, England, West Germany, and Holland have dominated the World Cup, which in soccer circles is regarded as more prestigious and competitive than its Olympic counterpart. Gellér, Kertész, and Orbán were the harbingers of a seemingly irreversible attrition. Since the middle of the 1960s there have been no outstanding Jewish soccer players in Hungary.

The respectable record of achievements which Jewish boxers had piled up in six of eleven weight divisions in the interwar period also fell apart. Only two notable exceptions, both confirming the sad reality, may be cited. Miksa Bondi, a four-time (1937-40) national flyweight champion, emerged from hiding, trained hard, and won his fifth and last championship as a bantamweight in 1948. The sole newcomer was the half-Jewish György Gedó, whose boxing career reached the pinnacle of success. A retiring young man from the provinces who seemed somewhat out of place in bustling Budapest, Gedó struggled to overcome a series of injuries on his way to the top. In the 1968 Olympic Games in Mexico City, he was forced to retire when his eyebrow split open in the first round. He rebounded to win two European championships (1969 Bucharest; 1971 Madrid). In the summer of 1972 he broke a finger on his left hand, yet he went on training for the approaching Munich Olympics. His unwavering determination, solid grasp of technique, and fierce attacking style helped him to overcome the psychological and physical pains of the injury and win the gold medal in the junior flyweight division.

One of the architects of boxing in the postwar reconstruction of that sport was Zsigmond Ádler. After months of hiding in a remote village waiting for the war to end, Ádler emerged to become the teacher to generations of young boxers, including László Papp, Hungary's three-time Olympic champion.

In addition to Gedó's career, the careers of two other half-Jewish athletes deserve to be mentioned. The combination of disciplined military training and arduous athletic preparation pushes the pentathlete to the limits of his mental concentration and physical ability. István Móna succeeded in reaching his limits in that exacting sport in the latter half of the 1960s. Both the national and international phases of his career were marked by success in team competition and its relative lack of individual achievement. The tall and powerful pentathlete was a member of the Bp. Honvéd, the team of the Hungarian armed forces, which won five consecutive national titles (1962-66). He was also a tireless and spirited contributor to the three-member national pentathlon team, which had a remarkable record of gold-medal performances in international competition, winning four world titles (1963, 1965-67), before reaching the Olympic pinnacle in 1968 in Mexico City. While Móna finished first in none of the national individual championships in which he competed, he once placed fourth (1966) and twice fifth (1963, 1965) in world individual competition.

Sixteen Olympic Games after Richárd Weisz became the first Hungarian wrestler to win a gold medal, Norbert Növényi performed the same feat. He was a relative newcomer among the world's top 90-kilo Greco-Roman wrestlers, still a junior champion in 1977. However, in 1979 the powerful Norbi established a reputation among the "adults" by finishing second in both the European and world championships. A determined and purposeful competitor, he cast an ambitious glance toward the Olympic gold. He became totally absorbed in training, in a single-minded commitment to achieving his goal. In May 1980 he won the national title in the 90-kilo division, which augured well for his prospects. In the competition at the rump Olympic Games in Moscow, Növényi overwhelmed his opponents with a formidable display of strength, speed, and technical skill. Having mauled the Romanian Dicu in the final, the twenty-three-year-old wrestler of the Bp. Dózsa kissed everyone in sight in a jubilant victory celebration of his Olympic prize.

In tennis Jewish contributions show a quantitiative decline in comparison with the interwar period. Only one player acquired more than national fame. After years of forced absence, Zsuzsa Körmöczy returned to competition and became the most successful and durable Hungarian player. She won a series of national championships (1945-46, 1950, 1958, 1961, 1963, singles; 1946, 1948, 1950, 1954, 1958, 1961, doubles; 1945-46, 1948, 1950, mixed doubles). She was a member of the Bp. Vasas Sport Klub, which with her help won eight national team titles. Körmöczy was one of the few Hungarian tennis players to acquire an international reputation. Though illness and injury frequently hampered her progress, she overcame obstacles with tenacity and willpower. A base-line specialist, her footwork and anticipation were exemplary. Her powerful forehand, consistent backhand, lobs, and passing shots were the undoing of many an outstanding serve-and-volley player. She was ranked second in the world in 1958. That was the pinnacle of her career. Of the nine tournaments she entered, Körmöczy won eight, including the French Open, and reached the semifinals at Wimbledon. Her last major victory on the European circuit was in 1962 at Monte Carlo, where she captured the women's singles title for the sixth time. In 1963 Körmöczy made it to the finals of the Italian Open, but was defeated by the American Althea Gibson. She also reached the semifinals of the French Open.

Achievements by men were much more modest. None compares favorably with Körmöczy's. András Káli and Péter Klein were members of the national team champion Bp. Dózsa. Káli played from 1957 to 1963; Klein from 1964 to 1978.

In chess two players acquired national prominence. Tibor Flórián (Feldman) won the national individual championship in 1945. Tibor Weinberger was a member of the Bp. Vörös Meteor in 1951, 1953, 1954, and 1956, when the team won national championships.

The dissolution of the *VAC* in 1947 had a disastrous effect on the participation of men in gymnastics. Only István Sárkány, an outstanding competitor of the 1930s, achieved results of note as a member of the 1949 national champion Munkás Testedző Egylet. Among the women too the fact that they were few in number was more than compensated for by excellence in quality. The career of Ágnes Keleti (Klein) is a case in point. Between 1947 and 1955 Keleti was the dominant force on the national scene. She accumulated national titles literally by the dozen: 1949-55, uneven bars; 1947-49, 1951-53, 1955 balance beam; 1945, 1948, 1950-51, hand apparatus; 1948, 1950, 1954, horse vault; 1947-55, floor exercise; 1947-48, rhythmic exercise; 1945, 1949-50, free exercise; 1947-55, combined exercises; and 1946-50, 1951, 1954, team. No less impressive was Keleti's performance in international competition, in which she represented Hungary twenty-four times between 1947 and 1956. A serious injury two days before she was to compete in the 1948 Olympic Games in London forced her to watch her teammates as a spectator. She recovered, resumed training, and soon returned to top form. In the World University Games of 1949 Keleti won four gold medals, a silver, and a bronze. It was a warmup for a greater test. In the Helsinki Olympics of 1952 Keleti won four medals: a gold (floor exercise), a silver (team), and two bronze (uneven bars and hand apparatus team), and placed fourth (balance beam) and sixth (combined exercises). If her performance was remarkable in 1952, it was to be overshadowed by an even more formidable display of talent, determination, and ability in the 1954 World Championship. She finished first on the uneven bars and the hand apparatus team, second in the combined team, and third on the balance beam. Nor would this performance be the high-water mark of her career. The pinnacle—and swan song—came in 1956. The thirty-five-year-old Keleti triumphed probably even beyond her most optimistic expectations. In the Melbourne Olympics she won four gold medals (uneven bars, balance beam, floor exercise, and hand apparatus team) and two silver medals (combined exercises and team). "I'm through for good," sighed an exhausted and misty-eyed Keleti. That declaration, as far as her career was concerned, was predictable, perhaps even overdue. However, Keleti was through in another, unexpected way as well. While the competition for the coveted Olympic medals was going on, the anti-Communist revolution raged in Hungary. Instead of resuming the pampered life of a sport legend in a socialist country, Keleti chose to defect. She settled in Israel and became a coach and a physical education instructor, imparting her enormous knowledge and experience to young gymnasts, for whom she is an ideal.

The other outstanding Jewish gymnast was Aliz Kertész, fourteen years Keleti's junior. Unlike Keleti, who had won forty-six individual titles and shared in seven team titles, Kertész left a more subdued legacy. She won only two national individual championships (uneven bars and balance beam, both in 1958) and was a member of the Bp. Honvéd, the Hungarian Army's team, which captured the national title in 1955 and 1956. Kertész was more successful in international competition, representing Hungary seventeen times between 1954 and 1958. In the 1954 World Gymnastics Championships in Rome she won two medals: a gold as a member of Hungary's winning team in the hand apparatus competition and a silver in the combined team competition. She also had considerable success in the World University Games of 1954, winning two gold and three silver medals. Kertész's second series of outstanding achievements took place at the 1956 Olympics. She was a member of Hungary's gold medal winning hand apparatus team, received a silver medal in the combined team standing and placed sixth on the uneven bars. The brutal Soviet intervention during the revolution notwithstanding, Kertész chose to return to Hungary with an Olympic team decimated by defection.

Fencing revealed a predictable imbalance. The combination of retirement and the tragic losses in the Holocaust all but wiped out the chain of brilliant Jewish fencers who had dominated the men's competition. Only two managed to revive the spark. Tamás Gábor was a two-time (1960-61) national épée champion and a member of the Bp. Vörös Meteor's four-time (1957-60) national champion épée team. A forty-nine-time member of Hungary's national épée team, he had a successful sixteen-year career on the international piste. In the 1954 World University Games he was a member of the Hungarian épée team that won the gold medal. He also established himself as a world-class competitor by winning six gold medals in world championship competition (one gold: 1959, team; three silvers: 1957-58, team, 1962, individual; two bronzes: 1961, individual, 1963, team). At the 1964 Olympic Games in Tokyo, Gábor was a member of Hungary's national team which won the gold medal and placed fourth in the épée individual event.

Sándor Erdős was Gábor's heir in the 1970s. He was a member of Hungary's gold medal épée team at the 1972 Olympic Games in Munich and the one that placed fourth at Montreal in 1976. His successes at world championship competition were even more extensive. He was a member of the Hungarian teams that won two gold medals (1970 and 1971), a silver (1973), and two bronzes (1974 and 1975). In individual competition his efforts were crowned with more modest success; he placed fourth in 1971.

Of the three outstanding women who played major roles in Hungary's remarkable postwar achievement in the foil competition, two, the Elek sisters, were holdovers from the interwar years. Ilona Elek, the winner of the gold medal in the individual foil event at the Berlin Olympics of 1936, was thirty-nine when she won the first of her five postwar national individual titles (1946-47, 1949-50, 1952) and the first of her three national team titles (1946, 1949-50). A fifty-three-time international between 1929 and 1956, Elek's performance in Olympic and world competition was even more impressive. Twelve years after her triumph in Nazi Germany, Elek overwhelmed her opponents with lightning-quick attacks in her quest to win a second Olympic gold in London. Her triumph became the springboard for a new series of remarkable achievements that culminated in the immensely exciting finals of the women's individual foil competition at the Helsinki Olympics of 1952. Elek and the Italian Irene Camber ended up in a tie, each with five victories. In the deciding round, Camber edged Elek by a score of 4-3. Thus by the narrowest of margins Elek failed to win her third Olympic gold. It became the most painful memory of her brilliant career. "My blood pressure still rises whenever I think of it," she admitted in an 1982 interview. Notwithstanding the bitter disappointment she went on to yet another series of triumphs. She had already won two gold medals in world championship competition (1937, team; 1951, individual), and three silver medals (1937, individual; 1948 and 1951, team). Again she decisively contributed to Hungarian team efforts (1952, 1953, and 1955, gold; 1956, bronze). In the individual competition, however, victory eluded her (1954, silver; 1955, bronze). All in all, Elek was the most successful competitor in the history of women's fencing, winning a staggering thirteen gold and six silver medals in Olympic, world, and European championships.

Ilona Elek's brilliant career overshadowed that of all of her contemporaries, including her sister's. Still, Margit Elek, three years her junior, was a great fencer in her own right. Margit trained and competed hard. She won no national individual titles, but she was a member of national championship teams in 1946, 1949, 1950, and 1954. She also performed well in international competition, representing Hungary fifty times in the course of a career that spanned a quarter of a century (1931-1957). In its postwar phase Elek could only place once in a major international competition. She finished sixth at the London Olympics of 1948. On the other hand her achievements in team competition remained consistently superior. She won twelve medals in world foil competition (1937, 1952-55, gold; 1948 and 1951, silver; 1956, bronze) and European competition (1933-35, gold; 1936, silver).

The last great Hungarian-Jewish fencer of the postwar period was Ildikó Rejtő. Despite a promising start—she won the junior world title in 1956 and 1957—the experts doubted that she would be able to conquer a slight hearing disability and become a truly exceptional competitor. She proved them wrong. Rejtő won her first national foil individual title at the age of twenty-one in 1958. She was subsequently national champion in 1961, 1962, 1969, 1970, and 1971. She was also a member of the Bp. Dózsa, the club whose team she helped win eight national championships. Rejtő's true mastery of the foil was more clearly evident in international competition, in which she represented Hungary over 150 times. For sheer medal count, Rejtő was a prolific collector. In world championship competition she won five golds (1959, 1962, 1967, 1973, team; 1963, individual), seven silvers (1961, 1963, 1966, 1971, 1974, 1975, team; 1971, individual), three bronzes (1969, team; 1957, 1973, individual). Rejtő's Olympic career also spanned sixteen years. Her most successful year was 1964. At the Toyko Olympics she triumphed in the women's foil individual competition and was a member of Hungary's gold-winning team. She also won three silver medals (1960, 1968, 1972, team) and two bronze medals (1973, individual; 1976, team). Rejtő's remarkable string of victories provided a reassuring continuity of Jewish contributions to fencing in Hungary. Unlike Ilona and Margit Elek, her predecessors, Rejtő was a product of Hungary's reconstructed sport structure, socialist and politicized.

The future of Hungarian-Jewish fencers is uncertain in the extreme. Neither Rejtő nor Tamás Gábor, the outstanding Jewish fencer of the 1960s, could pass on their swords to worthy heirs. Since their retirement there have been no world-class accomplishments by a Hungarian-Jewish fencer.

The best showing and densest concentration of Jews in the postwar era has been in the water sports. One of Hungary's most outstanding kayakers of the 1950s and 1960s was László Fábián. Competing with a variety of partners, Fábián was a dominant force in virtually all distances. Unlike the overwhelming majority of athletes, who must prove themselves on the national scene before they are allowed to represent their countries in international competition, Fábián competed on both levels almost simultaneously. In 1956 he won the first of his many national titles and his only gold medal at the Olympic Games in Melbourne, in the pairs 10,000-meter event. In the course of a career that spanned twelve years, Fábián triumphed in twenty-five national championships (pairs, 500 m. 1956; 1000 m. 1956-58, 1961-62; 10,000 m. 1956-64, 1967-68; fours, 1000 m. 1955, 1957, 1961-63; 10,000 m. 1954; river championship pairs, 1963; and fours, 1961-62) and won seventeen medals in international championships: twelve gold (Olympics, pairs 10,000 m. 1956; world pairs 10,000 m. 1958, 1963; fours and pairs, 1966; European, pairs, 500 m. 1957; 1000 and 10,000 m. 1961; 10,000 m. 1963; fours, 1963; pairs, 1965, 1967), three silvers (world, fours, 10,000 m. 1966; European, pairs, 10,000 m. 1957; fours, 1969), and two bronzes (European, pairs, 10,000 m. 1959; and 1000 m. 1965).

Among the prominent Hungarian canoeists only one Jewish competitor achieved national reputation. In the 1950s Imre Farkas won a series of national titles (pairs, 500 m. 1959-60; 1000 m. 1956-57; 10,000 m. 1956-57). Unlike Fábián's remarkable string of victories in international competition, Farkas's relatively brief career was devoid of memorable achievements outside Hungary.

It was perhaps fitting that a Jewish Olympic champion-turned-architect should have designed the structure that was to become a monument for some of the greatest and most memorable Jewish contributions to sports. The *Nemzeti Sportuszoda,* Hungary's famed swimming facility, was built in 1931 after the plans of Alfréd Hajós-Guttmann. Located on Margit Island in the Danube between Buda and Pest, it became the nerve center and training ground for coaches, swimmers, and water polo players who would eventually help Hungary to become the pacesetter in world standards.

When interviewed or in their autobiographies the luminaries of water sports frequently refer to the masters. They are the coaches who discovered them, charted their careers, and even molded their personalities. In water polo, a unique chain of Jewish coaches descended from the quintessential master, the legendary Béla Komjádi. He had been the chief architect of that sport and remained its principal inspirational force long after his premature death in 1933. Under Komjádi's captainship Hungary's national water polo team won an Olympic gold (1932) and finished first in three European championships (1926-7, 1931). Komjádi's legacy found two notable cultivators in the postwar period: Miklós Sárkány and Dezső Gyarmati, two Olympic champion water polo players-turned-coaches who further enriched Hungary's already brightly shining image in international competition. Though both are highly regarded for their tactical and practical expertise, neither Sárkány nor Gyarmati succeeded in equaling Komjádi's prestige and achievements.

The exact number of Jewish players of the postwar era cannot be determined. Two players, both half-Jewish, made valuable contributions to water polo in Hungary: Dezső Gyarmati and György Kárpáti. Both his teammates and the experts agree that the left-handed Gyarmati, affectionately nicknamed "Suta" ("lefty" or "clumsy"), was one of the greatest players of all time. He was the first truly complete player, outstanding on defense and a prolific scorer as well. Those who follow the game fondly recall that Gyarmati scored one of the most spectacular goals ever, from a distance of twenty-five meters, to Ottó Boros, whose domain was generally considered impregnable. He helped the two teams he successively played for to win an impressive number of national titles (Bp. Dózsa Sport Kör 1948, 1950-52, 1955; FTC 1962-63). Gyarmati was also the workhorse of Hungary's national team, on which he played 109 times. The high-water mark of his seventeen-year-long career was a string of remarkable achievements in international competition. He won medals at Olympic Games (gold, 1952, 1956, 1964; silver, 1948; bronze, 1960), European championships (gold, 1954, 1962), and World University Games (gold, 1947, 1949).

Róbert Antal's career as a goalie was hampered by his allegiance to a club—the *MTK*—that won no national titles. He was further impeded by being a contemporary of the non-Jewish László Jeney of the Vasas and subsequently the *FTC,* the preeminent Hungarian goalie of his time. Between 1948 and 1952 he was tapped for the national team six times, tending the goal of the "B" selection of second stringers. He capped his career by sharing in the victory of the gold medal winning Hungarian team at the 1952 Olympic Games at Helsinki. Although the thirty-one-year-old Jewish goalie did not play in the decisive matches he must have found consolation in the time-honored athletic adage, "A medal's a medal's a medal."

György Kárpáti was Gyarmati's younger contemporary, best friend, and teammate in the *FTC* and on the national team. Unlike Gyarmati, the muscular, small-statured Kárpáti was a powerful and agile swimmer. His speed made him a valuable member of the *FTC*'s freestyle relay teams, which won four national titles in the years he was a member (4 x 100 meters, 1959; 4 x 200 meters, 1956, 1958, 1960). He was a three-time international swimmer between 1956 and 1958 and swam for the national 4 x 100-meter freestyle relay teams that finished second (1963) and third (1961) at the World University Games. His principal allegiance, however, was to water polo. He was a lifelong member of the *FTC* water polo team, helping it to win four national titles (1962-63, 1965, 1968). Kárpáti seemed also to have reserved a permanent position on the national team; he represented Hungary 165 times in international competition between 1952 and 1969. Speed, agility, and ball handling kept Kárpáti in the limelight long after most water polo players prudently retire or are made to retire. He was only seventeen when he was selected for the national team and remained one of its stalwarts for over a decade. Kárpáti's medal collection includes three Olympic golds (1952, 1956, 1964) and a bronze (1960), and three golds for European championships (1954, 1958, and 1962), highlighting a career that was a model and an object of envy for contemporaries and successors alike.

Four other notable Jewish players, Sándor Kőszegi, Károly Gáti, Tamás Wiesner and Ferenc Salamon, were members of first-division teams. All except Salamon played at least once on the national team.

Jewish contributions to swimming in the postwar era were both well-founded and well-transmitted. There was, however, a surprising turnaround.

Whereas the outstanding prewar Jewish swimmers were almost exclusively men, the postwar generation consisted mostly of women. Much of Hungary's success in the women's competition in the early 1950s must be attributed to the indefatigable labors of Imre Sárosi, the Jewish "master." A coach since 1930, Sárosi has been the discoverer and principal coach of a number of Jewish swimmers who became Olympic, world, European, and national champions, such as Adél Vámos, Kató Szőke, Éva Székely, and her daughter, Andrea Gyarmati. "I'm married to swimming, that's why I didn't get married," the septuagenarian Sárosi noted in a recent interview. His "children" speak of him with love, admiration, and gratitude even as they recall the exhausting training schedule which he devised for them. He was a severe, fanatical taskmaster, who demanded total subordination to the punishing methods which he pioneered in Hungary, aimed at the development of strength and stamina. For his swimmers, Sárosi set three unchanging objectives: train hard, win consistently, and set records. He was spared the tragic fate which thousands of Jews in the military labor service suffered. He escaped in the confusion which the rapidly advancing Soviet armies caused among the German and Hungarian forces at the front. Soon after the liberation of Budapest in February 1945 Sárosi returned. Characteristically unfazed, he sought out his swimmers, some of whom had to walk five hours on rouble-filled streets to reach the pool. They trained hard even though they hardly had anything to eat. Sárosi's perseverance and determination soon paid off. On August 20 the first swimming meet of the postwar era was held in the rebuilt Sportuszoda. One of Sárosi's Jewish pupils, Éva Székely, won the women's 100-meter breaststroke, setting the first record in the postwar history of swimming in Hungary.

Székely's victory marked the appearance of a new generation of remarkable Jewish swimmers and the beginning of a string of unprecedented decade-long victories both in national and international competition. There has never been a more representative personality among the many outstanding Jewish contributors to sports in Hungary. Though few, if any, active or retired Jewish athletes were inclined to reveal their religious identity (German family names, some Hungarian family names combined with certain given names and membership in the *VAC* were to be sure instant clues to Jewish background), Székely took a courageous and determined stand in going public with her Jewishness. In the course of a nationally televised interview in 1974 she spoke of the anti-Jewish laws of the early 1940s which limited participation in athletic competition to those who could document non-Jewish origin as far back as their grandparents. "That was no problem for me," Székely noted. "I didn't have to go back as far as my grandparents. Unequivocally, I was a Jew."

Under Sárosi's direction Székely became one of Hungary's preeminent swimmers and one of the world's best. The years of forced absence had no visible effects on her. Though she had not been allowed to swim competitively or train in public, Székely retained her determination and remained in top physical shape by running up and down the stairs of the apartment building in which she and her family lived. However unorthodox, the conditioning paid off. She became an unusually versatile and prodigiously successful competitor soon after the war had ended. Among Hungary's postwar national champions she would be one of the most reliable and frequent repeaters.

Although Székely had won but one national title—river swimming relay in 1940—before the anti-Jewish laws removed her from the ranks of competitors, her unique talent, physical prowess, and unswerving determination soon yielded more than ample compensation. Between 1946 and 1954 she won 32 national individual titles (freestyle: 100 meters 1946-47, 1950; 200 m. 1946-51; 400 m. 1947-51; breaststroke: 100 m. 1946-48, 200 m. 1945-47; butterfly: 100 m. 1949-51, 1953-54; 200 m. 1949-51; medley: 200 m. 1949, 1951, 1953) and eleven national team titles (freestyle: 4 x 100 m. 1945, 1948-51, 1953-56; medley: 4 x 100 m. 1949, 1953).

Despite her versatility Székely's most memorable achievements were in the breaststroke, which she alternated with the butterfly, the first woman in Hungary to compete successfully in that style.

Soon "Madame Butterfly," as she was affectionately called, added an international dimension to her already well-established national reputation. In 1947 she won three gold medals at the World University Games and finished second in the 200-meter breaststroke in the European championship. Székely's first attempt to win Olympic laurels, however, ended in disappointment. In London she placed fourth in the 200-meter breaststroke and in the 4 x 100-meter freestyle. Tearful but resolute, Székely resumed the rigorous training under Sárosi's direction. Her string of national titles grew steadily; records fell to the relentless pace of her powerful strokes. At the 1951 World University Games Székely won five gold medals (1000-

meter freestyle, 100- and 200-meter butterfly, 4 x 100-meter freestyle, and 3 x 100-meter medley). The high-water mark of Székely's international career came in 1952. At the Olympic Games in Helsinki she won the gold medal in the 200-meter breaststroke with a new Olympic record.

The twenty-five-year-old Székely could have retired and become, like other Olympic champions, a permanent national institution. A pharmacist by profession, and married to Dezső Gyarmati, the Olympic champion water polo player, she gave birth in 1954 to a daughter, Andrea, who was to become another swimming champion and to whose upbringing she could have devoted her retirement. Instead, Székely pressed on. Her next objective was a repeat Olympic performance in Melbourne in 1956, where she swam in top form and where victory seemed all but assured. However, Hungary's participation in the Melbourne Olympics was adversely affected by the outbreak of the revolution in 1956. Repeating her best time, that of the 200-meter breaststroke in 1955, would have been enough to capture a second Olympic gold. However, Székely, fretting over the safety of her daughter in the beleaguered city, finished second to the German Ursula Happe. Family honor was partially recompensed when the Gyarmati-led water polo team shut out the Russians 4-0 and went on to win the gold medal. It was the most bitterly fought and bloodiest match in the history of the game.

In the chaotic aftermath of the revolution, the lure of the West, to which many Hungarian athletes had succumbed, proved irresistible to Hungary's most famous Olympic couple. In February 1957 Gyarmati, Székely, and their young daughter were permitted to visit Vienna, where they promptly defected annd flew to the United States at the urging of Székely's relatives. Both were to regret leaving the privileged status which socialist countries accord to outstanding athletes and returned to Budapest within a year and a half. They were divorced a few years thereafter.

In the aftermath of her memorable television interview in 1974, Székely turned to writing. Her published works, some short stories and a book, all autobiographical, have been enthusiastically received by Hungary's sport-loving readers. They serve, though not entirely by the author's design, a dual purpose. They may be regarded as important primary sources for sport history, they also stand as a unique testimony to a determined commitment to Jewish identity. Székely's first literary venture, a short story entitled "The True, Great Love of My Life in Water," was published in the

1977-78 Yearbook of the Jewish community, a highly acclaimed repository of scholarly articles and works of fiction. The story is devoid of clues to the author's religious affiliation, but her choice of publisher speaks for itself, albeit quietly. Székely's autobiography, *Only the Victor May Weep,* was an instant bestseller. Copies of the first edition were bought up within days. Her account of the events of 1944, the wearing of the yellow Star of David, and the experiences in an overcrowded apartment of a house under Swiss protection, leaves an indelible impression on the reader.

Székely's enduring fame, heightened by the popularity of her book and a number of high awards she received for her contributions to swimming, both as a competitor and a coach, tends to crowd out the successes that other Jewish luminaries among her contemporaries and successors have enjoyed.

One of the most unique careers in the women's freestyle in the early 1950s was that of Katalin Szőke. Her inclusion among Jewish athletes may raise some eyebrows, possibly hers above all. Still, she is the daughter of a Jewish mother, her namesake and the premier Hungarian backstroker of the late 1920s, even though her father, Márton Homonnai, a two-time (1932, 1936) Olympic gold-medalist water polo player, was a professing anti-Semite. Szőke assumed her mother's family name to avoid embarrassment. The most surprising feature of her brilliant, albeit brief career is the paucity of national individual titles. She won only two, in the 100 and 200 meters in 1954. Szőke's performance in the relays was more impressive. She shared in six national titles (4 x 100-meter freestyle, 1948, 1950, 1952; 4 x 100-meter medley, 1951-52, 1954). She was in top form. Indeed, 1954 looked like the watershed of her career. In international competition she won four gold medals (European championship, individual 100-meter freestyle, 4 x 100-meter freestyle relay; World University Games, 4 x 100-meter freestyle relay and 4 x 100-meter medley relay) and a silver (World University Games, 100-meter individual freestyle).

The pinnacle of Szőke's career, however, preceded these victories. It was at the 1952 Olympic Games in Helsinki that the seventeen-year-old swimmer gave the performance of her life. To be sure, being a member of Hungary's powerful, world record breaking 4 x 100-meter women's freestyle relay team in the early 1950s was a virtual guarantee of success in international competition. Thus, however gratified, few Hungarian swimming experts were unduly surprised when the team, with Szőke swimming the anchor leg, won the gold with a new world record, the only one in the entire swimming competition. The real shocker had come earlier. Szőke had not won an individual national title in the 100-meter freestyle, yet she placed fifth in the second heat of the Olympic qualifying rounds. In the final she swam in third place for most of the distance. With fifteen meters to go, she lunged into a furious finish, passing Johanna Termeulen of Holland and Judit Temes of Hungary, the reigning national champion, who had been given the best chance to win. Szőke's principal assets—unperturbability and explosiveness—netted her what undoubtedly was the most satisfying prize of her career.

Four years later in the Melbourne Olympics Hungary's women swimmers were overwhelmed by a group of spirited and talented Australian teenagers. Only the butterflier, twenty-nine-year-old Éva Székely, managed to capture second place in the 200-meter breaststroke. All were distracted by the revolution. Notwithstanding the privileged status which she had enjoyed in Hungary, Szőke chose to defect and accompanied other Hungarian Olympians who went to the United States. She now lives in California.

One of the premier Hungarian freestylers of the late 1950s and early 1960s was Mária Frank. She held nine national titles (100 meters, 1958-59; 200 meters, 1961-63; 400 meters, 1958, 1961-63), dominating all of the distances of her time. (The 800-meter event was added in 1965.) Frank also acquired a respectable reputation in international competition. She was a member of Hungary's 4 x 100-meter freestyle relay team that placed fourth in the Rome Olympics of 1960 and received the bronze in the same event in the 1962 European championships, where she also placed fifth in the 100-meter individual competition. She won a gold (4 x 100-meter freestyle relay) and two silver medals (100- and 400-meter individual freestyle) in the 1963 World University Games.

The career of the last great Hungarian-Jewish swimmer was actually foreordained by family tradition. Growing up as the only child of Hungary's most famous sports couple, she was to be surrounded by the trappings of privilege, popularity, and preferment. Her parents trophy collection of dozens of national titles and sixteen gold medals, acquired in Olympic, European, and World University championships, were a constant visual reminder to achieve. The path was clearly charted. Andrea Gyarmati the daughter of Dezső Gyarmati and Éva Székely, began training seriously at age twelve in 1966 under her mother's guidance. (By then her parents had been divorced for some years.) To the two styles, the butterfly and the freestyle, in which her mother excelled, she added the backstroke. Her progress was remarkably quick. Her achievements in national competition, considering her versatility, left little doubt that she was her parents' daughter. Between 1970 and 1973 Gyarmati amassed twenty-three individual titles (freestyle: 100 meters 1970-73, 200 m. 1971-73, 400 m. 1971-73; backstroke: 100 m. 1971-73, 200 m. 1970-73; butterfly: 100 m. 1970-73, 200 m. 1970-71) and set eleven national, nineteen European, and two world records.

Gyarmati plunged into the quest for international fame with the same sense of urgency, determination, and commitment. Her progress was even and the prospects looked promising. At the 1968 Olympic Games in Mexico City she placed fifth in the 100-meter freestyle and the 100-meter backstroke. She won three gold medals (100-meter butterfly, 1967 and 1969; 100-meter backstroke, 1969) and a silver (100-meter freestyle, 1970) in the junior European championships. In the European championships of 1970 she was a dominant force, capturing two titles (100-meter butterfly and 200-meter backstroke) and twice placing second (100-meter backstroke and the 4 x 100-meter freestyle relay). In Munich in 1972, however, Gyarmati's Olympic dream turned into a nightmare. In the preliminary heats with her parents looking on, she broke the world record in the 100-meter butterfly and had the fastest time among the qualifiers for the final of the 100-meter backstroke. However, the finals became a source of anguish and enduring disappointment for Gyarmati. She finished a heart-rendingly close second in the 100-meter backstroke and third in the 100-meter butterfly. Misfortune plagued her in the team competition too. Four years earlier the then-fourteen-year-old Gyarmati may have been pleased to have been chosen for the Hungarian Olympic swimming team, let alone to have helped it place fifth in the 4 x 100-meter freestyle relay. In Munich, being a member of a team that placed fourth only added to her disappointment. Still with her parents' support, Gyarmati rebounded and began training for the 1976 Olympic Games. The initial tests for success, however, proved inconclusive. At the 1973 world championships in Belgrade Gyarmati captured the bronze in the 200-meter backstroke and placed fourth in the 100 meters. Many world-class swimmers would have been delighted with such results, but for Gyarmati nothing less than total success sufficed.

In the spring of 1974 the twenty-year-old Gyarmati suddenly stopped in the middle of a training session supervised by her mother. "Mom," she said, "It's no fun anymore."

"I stopped the watch," Éva Székely recalls. "I stood up. Nothing more needed to be said. The stopwatch still shows the same time."

Married to Mihály Hesz, a dentist and former world and Olympic champion kayaker, Gyarmati is a pediatrician. She lives in Budapest.

Among the outstanding swimmers of the postwar era another group of Jewish women deserves recognition. Overshadowed by the achievements and reputation of world-class competitors and omitted from the statistics and biographies, some national titleholders and others known nationally have remained at the periphery of fame. Magda Felhős, a versatile competitor, was the national champion in the 200-meter individual medley in 1940 and a member of the 1946 4 x 100-meter freestyle national champion Magyar Munkás Úszó Egylet. Adél Vámos reached one of the high-water marks of her career in 1946 when she captured the national title in the 400-meter individual freestyle. The others came in 1945 and 1951 when she helped her team win the national championship in the 4 x 100-meter relay (she successively swam for the Újpesti Torna Egylet and the Lokomotív Sport Egyesület). Zsuzsa Nádor was also a member of the champion UTE team. Éva Pajor excelled in the backstroke. She was a two-time (1955-56) national champion in the 100 meters. The best known of this group of lesser luminaries was Vera Kárpáti, sister of the three-time Olympic and European champion water polo player György Kárpáti. In the late 1950s she was one of the best in the breaststroke. She won four national individual titles (200-meter breaststroke, 1957-58; 400-meter medley, 1957 and 1959) and was, surprisingly, a member of the 4 x 100-meter freestyle national champion relay team of the FTC.

EPILOGUE

Presently there appear to be no firm bases on which predictions about the future of Jewish contributions to Hungarian sports may be made with any reasonable measure of authority. It looks less than promising. Still, as an expression of confidence in the remarkable regenerative powers of Hungarian Jewry, concluding this work on a positive note may not be out of place. However, a vision of hope is neither nurtured by the reminders of outstanding Jewish athletic achievements of the past nor is it obfuscated by the seemingly irreversible waning of that tradition. Rather it circumvents both and receives inspiration from a third source.

Except for the all-Jewish membership of the *VAC* no area provides the historian a more reassuring hold on the reality of Jewish identity than one of the principal educational institutions of Hungarian Jewry. The Anna Frank Gimnázium, the only Jewish high school in Hungary, is an heir to a tradition of academic excellence and respect for physical education and sports which generations of pedagogues had created. The Budapesti Izraelita Hitközség Fiúgimnáziuma ("Boys High School of the Budapest Jewish Community"), as well as its counterpart for girls, opened its doors in 1919 following financial preparations that took a quarter of a century to complete. It not only survived but actually thrived in the boisterously demagogic anti-Semitic atmosphere of the interwar years. In addition to demonstrating convincing signs of a steady growth and acquiring an enviable academic reputation, the school accommodated students who displayed a lively interest in sports and physical education. In the dismal aftermath of the Second World War hundreds of students found within its walls a second home which, to some extent, provided the means for a transition from the horrible experiences of the Holocaust and the ensuing economic hardships and political uncertainties to an existence of dignity, sanity, and hope. However, by the late 1940s the school experienced a dramatic numerical decline due to illegal emigration and transfers to public schools. In an age when religious affiliation and middle-class background were regarded as obstacles to admission to universities, parents grew more and more disinclined to send their children to a school that was a guardian of both. The reversal of good fortune was a predictable consequence of the relentless social transformation, conducted in conformity to worker and peasant ideals and presided over by the Communist party under Mátyás Rákosi's servile Stalinist leadership. (Only slightly less lamentable is the spectacle of a self-perpetuating status quo, after the decline had leveled off, which Communist Party Chief János Kádár's experiment with an increasingly permissive form of Communism apparently forgot to address.)

In its heyday the "Zsidgim," as the school was affectionately called, occupied a building of massive size and impressive design that had a large, well-equipped gymnasium and an expansive courtyard where outdoor games were played. The excellent facilities, however, provided only the structural elements of an environment conducive to sports. True incentive and inspiration came from two physical education teachers whose images have been firmly etched in the recollection of generations of grateful and devoted graduates. Zoltán Dückstein dedicated his life and considerable pedagogical and technical expertise—he was a nationally and internationally respected gymnastics authority—to developing and training strong, healthy, and sport-loving Jewish students. His enthusiasm and friendly demeanor produced quick and lasting results. In addition to enthusiastically attending physical education classes, many students joined sport clubs or signed up for after-school instruction. The teams of the school became a force to contend with in Budapest's thriving high-school sports circuit. Still, students of exceptional athletic ability, such as István Sárkány, the *VAC*'s national champion gymnast in the 1930s, and Ferenc Salamon, a well-known first-division water polo player in the early postwar years, were rare.

In the bleak years of the Rákosi era János Strasser struggled to keep Dückstein's legacy alive. The odds against his succeeding were overwhelming. The overzealous guardians of the strictly controlled and supervised public school system, which formed the educational basis of an officially atheistic worker- and peasant-oriented society, noted that the number of students attending the "Zsidgim" had dropped from nearly a thousand to less than a hundred. They quickly resolved to nationalize the famed school building, whose facilities had indeed been designed to accommodate hundreds, not dozens. The boys' and girls' high schools were moved into an unused wing of the Országos Rabbiképző Intézet ("National Rabbinical Seminary") where even the much-reduced space seemed more than adequate. Once again the school became a refuge for the children of the outcasts of society, for students who had emerged from the nightmare of the Holocaust only to find themselves in the nightmare of Communism. Neither the prevailing conditions in the country nor the spartan surroundings augured well for the future of the school. Yet a handful of dedicated teachers continued to provide an education that was in the spirit of the distinguished academic tradition of the school. A small, ill-equipped gymnasium and a minuscule courtyard became Strasser's domain. Adroitly fusing discipline and enthusiasm, he revitalized the sagging morale of the few remaining athletically inclined students and developed a modest athletic program. It was a bittersweet reminder of what it had been in happier times. Teams were formed—mostly of the same students who signed up for different sports—and participated in regional tournaments in soccer, basketball, gymnastics, tennis, table tennis, athletics, and chess. Though victories in competition were few and far between, Strasser's accomplishments in the face of diminished enrollment and meager resources were nothing short of remarkable. His departure for the United States amid the confusion of the 1956 Revolution closed an inspiring chapter in the annals of the school.

Since then the vision of hope has dwindled. The lights are going out. Will the current custodians of the tradition succeed in saving at least the sparks? Failure will not be for the want of trying.

BIBLIOGRAPHICAL NOTE

Although a relatively small nation, Hungary has been a superpower in the world of sport. In fencing, water polo, pentathlon, table tennis, swimming, and soccer its athletes have reached uncommon heights, captured the imagination of experts and spectators alike, and established a lasting international reputation. The Hungarians' love of viewing and participating in sports is matched only by their delight in talking about them. It probably is the most popular topic of casual conversation on the street, at work, in cafés, and in the home. It is, however, no mere idle chatter. Hungarians are unusually knowledgeable about sports. They can cite long columns of statistics with flawless precision, recall the most minute details of noteworthy performances with uncommon flair for dramatic description, and are prepared to debate any point, wether it lends itself to controversy or not, with unflagging enthusiasm.

Knowledge of sports, however, goes beyond the physical experience. Hungarians love to read. They take special pride in books, most of which sell out within weeks after publication. Newspapers and magazines are read with similar relish.

Sport is among the most highly ranked topics on the list of reading priorities. The range of books and articles from which readers may select is unusually wide and varied. The authors represent an equally broad spectrum of experiences and expertise. They may be sport historians, outstanding former athletes, officials, journalists, and professional writers.

129

Their output is vast and growing so rapidly that no researcher of sports in Hungary need be disappointed by the lack of available and useful sources.

Unfortunately, these sources were of limited use in the preparation of this book. The principal obstacle turned out to be neither the difficulty which the Hungarian language presents to those unfamiliar with it, nor the Marxist analysis and verbiage that make even the most thoroughly researched work a stylistic nightmare and a challenge to credulity. Rather, the trouble was the institutionalized policy of keeping the religious origin of athletes out of public consciousness. The publications of the Jewish community are of little or not utility. The works of Jewish authors betray not even the slightest trace of acknowledgment of, let alone pride in, the achievements of Jewish athletes. The sole exception is an outdated one: Péter Ujvári, ed. *Magyar zsidó lexikon* [Hungarian-Jewish Lexicon] (Budapest, 1929), which lists some of the most outstanding Jewish contributions to sports in Hungary. Similarly, of limited utility is Bernard Postal, Jesse Silver, and Roy Silver, *The Encyclopedia of Jews in Sports* (New York: Bloch, 1965). It is incomplete and at times inaccurate, and served only as a stopgap.

Surprisingly, the most important sources turned out to be the ones on whose utility only slight hopes had been pinned. Interviews with former champions proved a curious experience. Memories must be tapped carefully, for while some athletes showed remarkable recollective powers, others could not remember or were simply mistaken. At times it was necessary to exercise caution. However, of the many avenues of oral communication some led to reliable sources that could corroborate established Jewish identities and in some cases identify athletes as Jews for the first time. The facts were embroidered with stories as the Jewish grapevine, that unique source of information, again proved its timeless utility. Still, striving for completeness remains a quest for the unattainable.

Those whose contributions were of the greatest importance were Éva Székely, István Sárkány, László Bellák, and Sándor Loewy. In addition to relating many interesting details of their outstanding careers, their familiarity with athletes in their respective sport as well as those outside it was of fundamental utility in the laborious and often frustrating task of identifying Jewish athletes or providing corroborating evidence.

Gradually the list of names began to take shape. Only then did the true scope and utility of Hungarian sport literature become evident. In it, for the preparation of this book, three broad areas were recognized.

First, for statistical information about the achievement and club affiliation of Jewish athletes three useful compendia were consulted. Tibor Sass, István László, and Zoltán Antal, eds. *A magyar sport kézikönyve* [Handbook of Hungarian Sport] (Budapest: Sport, 1960) and its second revised and expanded edition (Budapest: Sport, 1972) provide not only detailed and accurate statistics for all competitive sports but useful, albeit brief, historical overviews as well. The particular virtue of these works is that they are both comprehensive and definitive sources of information. In addition to the results of national competitions they list the achievements of Hungarian athletes in European, world, and Olympic championships. A more recent work is László Havas, *A magyar sport aranykönyve* [The Golden Book of Hungarian Sport] (Budapest: Sport, 1982). Its scope is roughly that of the former. However, whereas Havas omits the results of national championships he pays particular attention—in addition to European, world, and Olympic results—to the statistics of the World University Games, the under-twenty-one competition, and the European Cup.

Historians accustomed to Western scholarship will find the second category of Hungarian sport literature disconcerting. They might wish to approach it with circumspection, and it requires a heightened level of intellectual tolerance. The category is that of Marxist analysis and interpretation. However, the list of comprehensive works by Hungarian sport historians that fall in this category is mercifully short. Most are variants of and all are dependent on Éva Földes, László Kun, and László Kutassi, *A magyar testnevelés és sport története* [History of Hungarian Physical Education and Sport] (Budapest: Sport, 1977; 2d. ed., 1982). The authors afford a commendably broad chronological sweep from the ninth-century exploits of the wandering Magyar tribes to the present. However, their commitment to correlate the subject matter to socioeconomic peculiarities produces a predictable monotony in interpretation and a dutiful criticism of the pre-Communist period. There is generally a fulsome overview of the policies, institutions, and achievements that have charted the development of the Communist experiment in Hungary since 1948. Indeed it is lamentable that a work which is more suited to propagating a rigid ideology than to meeting the specifics of scholarship should be the sole comprehensive source of information for the unsuspecting researcher. Similar flaws are evident in some of the less pretentious and useful studies, such as László Kun and Attila Sipos, *A sport Magyaror-szágon* [Sport in Hungary] (Budapest: Kossuth, 1979; Jenő Boskovics, *The History of Hungarian Sport* (Budapest: Corvina, 1983), and József Vető, *Sports in Hungary* (Budapest: Corvina, 1965).

A welcome alternative to the current crop of Hungarian sport historians is provided by the late prolific and erudite Ferenc Mező. His indefatigable pursuit of pure scholarship for over half an eventful century, his cosmopolitan perspective, and gently flowing, anecdotal style make the reading of his numerous works a refreshing experience. Though best known for his work on the Olympic Games—its history earned him a gold medal in the epics category competition at the Ninth Olympiad in Amsterdam (1928)—Mező also authored a number of books on the history of sports in Hungary, such as *Képek a magyar sport multjából* [Pictures from the Past of Hungarian Sport] (Budapest, 1926); *A magyar sport multja és jelenje* [The Past and Present of Hungarian Sport] (Budapest, 1931); *Magyarok az olimpián* [Hungarians at the Olympics] (Budapest, 1932); and *Negyven év a magyar sport multjából* [Forty Years from the Past of Hungarian Sport] (Budapest, 1935). Mező's works stand as reminders that not all Hungarian historians used the tools of their profession to become ideologues.

By far the most engaging of the books on sports have been written by journalists, officials, and athletes. Unpretentious and unencumbered by the obligatory gestures of conformity to the Marxist overview, they are a virtually inexhaustible repository of treasures which range from accounts of major happenings to recollections of insignificant personal quirks, the kind of hodgepodge of information that delights the gossipy fan and the serious researcher alike. Character traits quickly come into view. Some are serious, perhaps excessively so as they stumble toward the dramatic; others are genuinely humorous, being either disconcertingly pompous or engagingly self-depreciatory. A few are simply tedious. Still, their aim is firm and they rarely miss their mark. Whether the objective is to inform, to set the record straight, or to redeem the author through emotional bouts of self-therapy, the product of their labor is not only instant entertainment but also a peephole to the world of super-athletes, which star-struck fans are ever ready to explore.

The most written-about sport in Hungarian sport literature is soccer, the most popular national pastime. However, as the remnants of Hungarian

Jewry staggered out of the nightmare of the Holocaust it became evident
that the once active Jewish presence in soccer had been virtually termin-
ated. Thus the utility of the works by Hungarian authors in that sport is
limited to the period before the Second World War. Information about
outstanding Jewish soccer players may be found in Zoltán Antal and
József Hoffer, *Alberttől Zsákig* [From Albert to Zsák] (Budapest: Sport,
1968); József Vedres, ed., *Az MTK 75 éve* [The 75 Years of the *MTK*]
(Budapest: Sport, 1963); László Rejtő, *Kilenc klub krónikája* [The Chronicle of Nine Clubs] (Budapest: Sport, 1969); Béla Nagy, *Fradisták: Az
FTC labdarúgói, 1900-1980* [Fradists: The Soccer Players of the *FTC,*
1900-1980] (Budapest: Sportpropaganda, 1981); János Major, Béla
Nagy, and László Szücs, *Fradi labdarúgó-szakosztály története* [History
of Fradi's Soccer Department] (Budapest: Sportpropaganda, 1972), and
László Rejtő, László Lukács, and György Szepesi, *Felejthetetlen 90
percek* [Unforgettable 90 Minutes] (Budapest: Sport, 1977).

In other sports the tradition also seems irremediably broken. The inexplicable paucity of works on track and field events, some of which
belong to the more popular sports in Hungary, made it necessary to gather
the data piecemeal fashion. Three sources yielded enough information to
provide convincing proof of the extensive Jewish participation and notable achievements. The "Atlétika" entry in the *Magyar zsidó lexikon,*
the ever-trustworthy grapevine, which turned out to be the richest vein of
all; and *Az MTK 75 éve*—the majority of Jewish athletes were members
of the *MTK*—which contains many interesting stories that add a unique
personal touch to the somewhat monotonous statistical tables. The "Bir-
kózás" (Wrestling) entry in the *Magyar zsidó lexikon* and the above two
sources document the emergence and success of Jewish wrestlers. In addition useful information may be extracted from Zoltán Syposs's anecdotal
Ez a szép játék [This Fine Game] (Budapest: Sport, 1976), which contains short biographies of Richárd Weisz and Ödön Radvány, two of the
greatest Jewish wrestlers.

No better reception awaits the researcher in the accessible literature
on table tennis. Two of the three sources used for track and field may
be of help. Unfortunately the *Magyar zsidó lexikon* has no entry on table
tennis. Instead the biographical portions of Victor Barna's entertaining
Table Tennis Today (London: Arthur Baker, 1962) may be consulted. The
memory of a few Jewish boxers is preserved in Béla Abody, *Kesztyüs kéz-
zel* [With Gloved Hands] (Budapest: Sport, 1982).

Only in four sports was the Holocaust bridged over. The losses were high, yet those who were left assured a fragile transition and led to a guarded recovery. The literary backdrop of these sports reflects the promise of progress that comes from survival, however painful.

Water sports—swimming and water polo—have attracted knowledgeable chroniclers, many of whom have been successful competitors. The most informative. of the works on swimming are: István Bárány, *A magyar úszósport útja* [The Path of Hungarian Water Sport] (Budapest: Sport, 1955); and Éva Székely, *Sírni csak a győztesnek szabad!* [Only the Winner May Weep!] (Budapest: Magvető, 1982). The last, one of the surprise best sellers in the year of its publication, is the autobiography of the great Jewish swimming champion. The authors of the best works on water polo are former players: Pál Peterdi, *Ó, póló. . . ! Vallomások labdáról, vízről, játékról* [O Polo . . . ! Conferssions about Ball, Water and Game] (Budapest: Sport, 1980), György Kárpáti, *Itt állok megfürödve* [I'm Left High and Dry] (Budapest: Author's Edition, 1981) and idem, *Medencék, játék, pofonok* [Pools, Goals, Slaps] (Budapest: Sport, 1982). The authors are knowledgeable and provide expert commentary. However, their style is disconcertingly chatty and the humor that pervades the books is often labored and tedious. For a comprehensive study of the prewar period see Lajos Pánczél, *A magyar vizipóló története* [History of Hungarian Water Polo] (Budapest, 1924).

Access to the history of gymnastics in Hungary is limited by the paucity of sources. Only two works provide anything more than statistics: Zoltán Dückstein, *Művészi és versenytorna* [Artistic and Competitive Gymnastics] (Budapest, 1935); and Sándor Dávid, *Szaltószabadság* [Freedom by Somersault] (Budapest: Sport, 1981).

A similar problem confronts the researcher in tennis. Pál Szőke's *100 éves a magyar tenisz* [Hungarian Tennis is a Hundred Years Old] (Budapest: OTSH, 1980) is virtually the only comprehensive account of the development of that sport in Hungary.

The best-documented of the transitive sports is fencing. Much of the credit for this must go to Zoltán Syposs, an eloquent and entertaining chronicler of sports and a keen-eyed biographer of outstanding athletes. His *Villanó pengék* [Flashing Blades] (Budapest: Sport, 1975) is a valuable source of information about the best Hungarian fencers and their achievements. Of lesser utility are Rudolf Kárpáti, *Karddal a világ körül*

[Around the World by Sword] (Budapest: Sport, 1965); and Béla Bay and Anna L. Réti, *A páston és páston kívül* [On and Beyond the Piste] (Budapest: Sportpropaganda, 1979). The tragic fate of Attila Petschauer, the great Jewish fencer of the 1930s, is the subject of Ottó Hámori, *Egy kardforgató élete* [A Swordsman's Life] (Budapest: Sportpropaganda, 1983).

As places of last refuge, Hungarian sport magazines and periodicals, such as *Képes Sport, Népsport,* the annual *A magyar sport évkönyve* [Yearbook of Hungarian Sport] and the selected publications of sport associations and the Testnevelési Főiskola ("College of Physical Education") may suffice. A somewhat outdated yet sill useful guide for most accessible sources (being the only such compendium) is Ferenc Krasovec, ed. *Válogatott testnevelés- és sporttörténeti bibliográfia* [Selected Bibliography of Physical Education and Sport History] (Budapest: n.d.). A more up-to-date but limited view of current works is provided by the annual editions of the *Szakirodalmi gyorstájékoztató* [Express Bibliography of Technical Literature] of the Testnevelési Főiskola.

INDEX

EAST EUROPEAN MONOGRAPHS

The *East European Monographs* comprise scholarly books on the history and civilization of Eastern Europe. They are published under the editorship of Stephen Fischer-Galati, in the belief that these studies contribute substantially to the knowledge of the area and serve to stimulate scholarship and research.

1. *Political Ideas and the Enlightenment in the Romanian Principalities, 1750–1831.* By Vlad Georgescu. 1971.
2. *America, Italy and the Birth of Yugoslavia, 1917–1919.* By Dragan R. Zivjinovic. 1972.
3. *Jewish Nobles and Geniuses in Modern Hungary.* By William O. McCagg, Jr. 1972.
4. *Mixail Soloxov in Yugoslavia: Reception and Literary Impact.* By Robert F. Price. 1973.
5. *The Historical and Nationalist Thought of Nicolae Iorga.* By William O. Oldson. 1973.
6. *Guide to Polish Libraries and Archives.* By Richard C. Lewanski. 1974.
7. *Vienna Broadcasts to Slovakia, 1938–1939: A Case Study in Subversion.* By Henry Delfiner. 1974.
8. *The 1917 Revolution in Latvia.* By Andrew Ezergailis. 1974.
9. *The Ukraine in the United Nations Organization: A Study in Soviet Foreign Policy. 1944–1950.* By Konstantin Sawczuk. 1975.
10. *The Bosnian Church: A New Interpretation.* By John V. A. Fine, Jr., 1975.
11. *Intellectual and Social Developments in the Habsburg Empire from Maria Theresa to World War I.* Edited by Stanley B. Winters and Joseph Held. 1975.
12. *Ljudevit Gaj and the Illyrian Movement.* By Elinor Murray Despalatovic. 1975.
13. *Tolerance and Movements of Religious Dissent in Eastern Europe,* Edited by Bela K. Kiraly. 1975.
14. *The Parish Republic: Hlinka's Slovak People's Party, 1939–1945.* By Yeshayahu Jelinek. 1976.
15. *The Russian Annexation of Bessarabia, 1774–1828.* By George F. Jewsbury. 1976.
16. *Modern Hungarian Historiography.* By Steven Bela Vardy. 1976.
17. *Values and Community in Multi-National Yugoslavia.* By Gary K. Bertsch. 1976.
18. *The Greek Socialist Movement and the First World War: the Road to Unity.* By George B. Leon. 1976.
19. *The Radical Left in the Hungarian Revolution of 1848.* By Laszlo Deme. 1976.
20. *Hungary between Wilson and Lenin: The Hungarian Revolution of 1918–1919 and the Big Three.* By Peter Pastor. 1976.

21. *The Crises of France's East-Central European Diplomacy, 1933-1938.* By Anthony J. Komjathy. 1976.

22. *Polish Politics and National Reform, 1775-1788.* By Daniel Stone. 1976.

23. *The Habsburg Empire in World War I.* Edited by Robert A. Kann, Bela K. Kiraly, and Paula S. Fichtner. 1977.

24. *The Slovenes and Yugoslavism, 1890-1914.* By Carole Rogel. 1977.

25. *German-Hungarian Relations and the Swabian Problem.* By Thomas Spira. 1977.

26. *The Metamorphosis of a Social Class in Hungary During the Reign of Young Franz Joseph.* By Peter I. Hidas. 1977.

27. *Tax Reform in Eighteenth Century Lombardy.* By Daniel M. Klang. 1977.

28. *Tradition versus Revolution: Russia and the Balkans in 1917.* By Robert H. Johnston. 1977.

29. *Winter into Spring: The Czechoslovak Press and the Reform Movement 1963-1968.* By Frank L. Kaplan. 1977.

30. *The Catholic Church and the Soviet Government, 1939-1949.* By Dennis J. Dunn. 1977.

31. *The Hungarian Labor Service System, 1939-1945.* By Randolph L. Braham. 1977.

32. *Consciousness and History: Nationalist Critics of Greek Society 1897-1914.* By Gerasimos Augustinos. 1977.

33. *Emigration in Polish Social and Political Thought, 1870-1914.* By Benjamin P. Murdzek. 1977.

34. *Serbian Poetry and Milutin Bojic.* By Mihailo Dordevic. 1977.

35. *The Baranya Dispute: Diplomacy in the Vortex of Ideologies, 1918-1921.* By Leslie C. Tihany. 1978.

36. *The United States in Prague, 1945-1948.* By Walter Ullmann. 1978.

37. *Rush to the Alps: The Evolution of Vacationing in Switzerland.* By Paul P. Bernard. 1978.

38. *Transportation in Eastern Europe: Empirical Findings.* By Bogdan Mieczkowski. 1978.

39. *The Polish Underground State: A Guide to the Underground, 1939-1945.* By Stefan Korbonski. 1978.

40. *The Hungarian Revolution of 1956 in Retrospect.* Edited by Bela K. Kiraly and Paul Jonas. 1978.

41. *Boleslaw Limanowski (1935-1935): A Study in Socialism and Nationalism.* By Kazimiera Janina Cottam. 1978.

42. *The Lingering Shadow of Nazism: The Austrian Independent Party Movement Since 1945.* By Max E. Riedlsperger. 1978.

43. *The Catholic Church, Dissent and Nationality in Soviet Lithuania.* By V. Stanley Vardys. 1978.

44. *The Development of Parliamentary Government in Serbia.* By Alex N. Dragnich. 1978.

45. *Divide and Conquer: German Efforts to Conclude a Separate Peace, 1914-1918.* By L. L. Farrar, Jr. 1978.

46. *The Prague Slav Congress of 1848.* By Lawrence D. Orton. 1978.

47. *The Nobility and the Making of the Hussite Revolution.* By John M. Klassen. 1978.

48. *The Cultural Limits of Revolutionary Politics: Change and Continuity in Socialist Czechoslovakia.* By David W. Paul. 1979.

49. *On the Border of War and Peace: Polish Intelligence and Diplomacy in 1937-1939 and the Origins of the Ultra Secret.* By Richard A. Woytak. 1979.

50. *Bear and Foxes: The International Relations of the East European States 1965-1969.* By Ronald Haly Linden. 1979.

51. *Czechoslovakia: The Heritage of Ages Past.* Edited by Ivan Volgyes and Hans Brisch. 1979.

52. *Prime Minister Gyula Andrassy's Influence on Habsburg Foreign Policy.* By Janos Decsy. 1979.

53. *Citizens for the Fatherland: Education, Educators, and Pedagogical Ideals in Eighteenth Century Russia.* By J. L. Black. 1979.

54. *A History of the "Proletariat": The Emergence of Marxism in the Kingdom of Poland, 1870-1887.* By Norman M. Naimark. 1979.

55. *The Slovak Autonomy Movement, 1935-1939: A Study in Unrelenting Nationalism.* By Dorothea H. El Mallakh. 1979.

56. *Diplomat in Exile: Francis Pulszky's Political Activities in England, 1849-1860.* By Thomas Kabdebo. 1979.

57. *The German Struggle Against the Yugoslav Guerrillas in World War II: German Counter-Insurgency in Yugoslavia, 1941-1943.* By Paul N. Hehn. 1979.

58. *The Emergence of the Romanian National State.* By Gerald J. Bobango. 1979.

59. *Stewards of the Land: The American Farm School and Modern Greece.* By Brenda L. Marder. 1979.

60. *Roman Dmowski: Party, Tactics, Ideology, 1895-1907.* By Alvin M. Fountain, II. 1980.

61. *International and Domestic Politics in Greece During the Crimean War.* By Jon V. Kofas. 1980.

62. *Fires on the Mountain: The Macedonian Revolutionary Movement and the Kidnapping of Ellen Stone.* By Laura Beth Sherman. 1980.

63. *The Modernization of Agriculture: Rural Transformation in Hungary, 1848-1975.* Edited by Joseph Held. 1980.

64. *Britain and the War for Yugoslavia, 1940-1943.* By Mark C. Wheeler. 1980.

65. *The Turn to the Right: The Ideological Origins and Development of Ukrainian Nationalism, 1919-1929.* By Alexander J. Motyl. 1980.

66. *The Maple Leaf and the White Eagle: Canadian-Polish Relations, 1918-1978.* By Aloysius Balawyder. 1980.

67. *Antecedents of Revolution: Alexander I and the Polish Congress Kingdom, 1815-1825.* By Frank W. Thackeray. 1980.

68. *Blood Libel at Tiszaeszlar.* By Andrew Handler. 1980.

69. *Democratic Centralism in Romania: A Study of Local Communist Politics.* By Daniel N. Nelson. 1980.

70. *The Challenge of Communist Education: A Look at the German Democratic Republic.* By Margrete Siebert Klein. 1980.

71. *The Fortifications and Defense of Constantinople.* By Byron C. P. Tsangadas. 1980.

72. *Balkan Cultural Studies.* By Stavro Skendi. 1980.

73. *Studies in Ethnicity: The East European Experience in America.* Edited by Charles A. Ward, Philip Shashko, and Donald E. Pienkos. 1980.

74. *The Logic of "Normalization:" The Soviet Intervention in Czechoslovakia and the Czechoslovak Response.* By Fred Eidlin. 1980.

75. *Red Cross, Black Eagle: A Biography of Albania's American Schol.* By Joan Fultz Kontos. 1981.

76. *Nationalism in Contemporary Europe.* By Franjo Tudjman. 1981.

77. *Great Power Rivalry at the Turkish Straits: The Montreux Conference and Convention of 1936.* By Anthony R. DeLuca. 1981.

78. *Islam Under the Double Eagle: The Muslims of Bosnia and Hercegovina, 1878-1914.* By Robert J. Donia. 1981.

79. *Five Eleventh Century Hungarian Kings: Their Policies and Their Relations with Rome.* By Z. J. Kosztolnyik. 1981.

80. *Prelude to Appeasement: East European Central Diplomacy in the Early 1930's.* By Lisanne Radice. 1981.

81. *The Soviet Regime in Czechoslovakia.* By Zdenek Krystufek. 1981.

82. *School Strikes in Prussian Poland, 1901–1907: The Struggle Over Bilingual Education.* By John J. Kulczychi. 1981.

83. *Romantic Nationalism and Liberalism: Joachim Lelewel and the Polish National Idea.* By Joan S. Skurnowicz. 1981.

84. *The "Thaw" In Bulgarian Literature.* By Atanas Slavov. 1981.

85. *The Political Thought of Thomas G. Masaryk.* By Roman Szporluk. 1981.

86. *Prussian Poland in the German Empire, 1871–1900.* By Richard Blanke. 1981.

87. *The Mazepists: Ukrainian Separatism in the Early Eighteenth Century.* By Orest Subtelny. 1981.

88. *The Battle for the Marchlands: The Russo-Polish Campaign of 1920.* By Adam Zamoyski. 1981.

89. *Milovan Djilas: A Revolutionary as a Writer.* By Dennis Reinhartz. 1981.

90. *The Second Republic: The Disintegration of Post-Munich Czechoslovakia, October 1938-March 1939.* By Theodore Prochazka, Sr. 1981.

91. *Financial Relations of Greece and the Great Powers, 1832–1862.* By Jon V. Kofas. 1981.

92. *Religion and Politics: Bishop Valerian Trifa and His Times.* By Gerald J. Bobango. 1981.

93. *The Politics of Ethnicity in Eastern Europe.* Edited by George Klein and Milan J. Reban. 1981.

94. *Czech Writers and Politics.* By Alfred French. 1981.

95. *Nation and Ideology: Essays in Honor of Wayne S. Vucinich.* Edited by Ivo Banac, John G. Ackerman, and Roman Szporluk. 1981.

96. *For God and Peter the Great: The Works of Thomas Consett, 1723–1729.* Edited by James Cracraft. 1982.

97. *The Geopolitics of Leninism.* By Stanley W. Page. 1982

98. *Karel Havlicek (1821–1856): A National Liberation Leader of the Czech Renascence.* By Barbara K. Reinfeld. 1982.

99. *Were-Wolf and Vampire in Romania.* By Harry A. Senn. 1982.

100. *Ferdinand I of Austria: The Politics of Dynasticism in the Age of Reformation.* By Paula Sutter Fichtner. 1982

101. *France in Greece During World War I: A Study in the Politics of Power.* By Alexander S. Mitrakos. 1982.

102. *Authoritarian Politics in a Transitional State: Istvan Bethlen and the Unified Party in Hungary, 1919–1926.* By William M. Batkay. 1982.

103. *Romania Between East and West: Historical Essays in Memory of Constantin C. Giurescu.* Edited by Stephen Fischer-Galati, Radu R. Florescu and George R. Ursul. 1982.

104. *War and Society in East Central Europe: From Hunyadi to Rakoczi— War and Society in Late Medieval and Early Modern Hungary.* Edited by János Bak and Béla K. Király. 1982.

105. *Total War and Peace Making: A Case Study on Trianon.* Edited by Béla K. Király, Peter Pastor, and Ivan Sanders. 1982

106. *Army, Aristocracy, and Monarchy: Essays on War, Society, and Government in Austria, 1618–1780.* Edited by Wayne S. Vucinich. 1982.

107. *The First Serbian Uprising, 1804–1813.* Edited by Wayne S. Vucinich. 1982.

108. *Propaganda and Nationalism in Wartime Russia: The Jewish Anti-Fascist Committee in the USSR, 1941–1948.* By Shimon Redich. 1982.

109. *One Step Back, Two Steps Forward: On the Language Policy of the Communist Party of Soviet Union in the National Republics.* By Michael Bruchis. 1982.

110. *Bessarabia and Bukovina: The Soviet-Romanian Territorial Dispute.* by Nicholas Dima. 1982

111. *Greek-Soviet Relations, 1917–1941.* By Andrew L. Zapantis. 1982.

112. *National Minorities in Romania: Change in Transylvania.* By Elemer Illyes. 1982.

113. *Dunarea Noastra: Romania, the Great Powers, and the Danube Question, 1914–1921.* by Richard C. Frucht. 1982.

114. *Continuity and Change in Austrian Socialism: The Eternal Quest for the Third Way.* By Melanie A. Sully. 1982

115. *Catherine II's Greek Prelate: Eugenios Voulgaris in Russia, 1771–1806.* By Stephen K. Batalden. 1982.

116. *The Union of Lublin: Polish Federalism in the Golden Age.* By Harry E. Dembkowski. 1982.

117. *Heritage and Continuity in Eastern Europe: The Transylvanian Legacy in the History of the Romanians.* By Cornelia Bodea and Virgil Candea. 1982.

118. *Contemporary Czech Cinematography: Jiri Menzel and the History of The "Closely Watched Trains".* By Josef Skvorecky. 1982.

119. *East Central Europe in World War I: From Foreign Domination to National Freedom.* By Wiktor Sukiennicki. 1982.

120. *City, Town, and Countryside in the Early Byzantine Era.* Edited by Robert L. Hohlfelder. 1982.

121. *The Byzantine State Finances in the Eighth and Ninth Centuries.* By Warren T. Treadgold. 1982.

122. *East Central European Society and War in Pre-Revolutionary Eighteenth Century.* Edited by Gunther E. Rothenberg, Bela K. Kiraly and Peter F. Sugar. 1982.

123. *Czechoslovak Policy and the Hungarian Minority, 1945–1948.* By Kalman Janics. 1982.

124. *At the Brink of War and Peace: The Tito-Stalin Split in a Historic Perspective.* Edited by Wayne S. Vucinich. 1982.

125. *The Road to Bellapais: The Turkish Cypriot Exodus to Northern Cyprus.* By Pierre Oberling. 1982.

126. *Essays on World War I: Origins and Prisoners of War.* Edited by Peter Pastor and Samuel R. Williamson, Jr. 1983.

127. *Panteleimon Kulish: A Sketch of His Life and Times.* By George S. N. Luckyj. 1983.

128. *Economic Development in the Habsburg Monarchy in the Nineteenth Century: Essays.* Edited by John Komlos. 1983.

129. *Warsaw Between the World Wars: Profile of the Capital City in a Developing Land, 1918–1939.* By Edward D. Wynot, Jr. 1983.

130. *The Lust for Power: Nationalism, Slovakia, and The Communists, 1918–1948.* By Yeshayahu Jelinek. 1983.

131. *The Tsar's Loyal Germans: The Riga German Community: Social Change and the Nationality Question, 1855–1905.* By Anders Henriksson. 1983.

132. *Society in Change: Studies in Honor of Bela K. Kiraly.* Edited by Steven Bela Vardy. 1983.

133. *Authoritariansim in Greece: The Metaxas Regime.* By Jon V. Kofas. 1983.

134. *New Hungarian Peasants: An East Central European Experience with Collectivization.* Edited by Marida Hollos and Bela C. Maday. 1983.

135. *War, Revolution, and Society in Romania: The Road to Independence.* Edited by Ilie Ceausescu. 1983.

136. *The Beginning of Cyrillic Printing, Cracow, 1491: From the Orthodox Past in Poland.* By Szczepan K. Zimmer. 1983.

137. *Effects of World War I. The Class War After the Great War: The Rise of Communist Parties in East Central Europe, 1918–1921.* Edited by Ivo Banac. 1983.

138. *Bulgaria 1878–1918. A History.* By Richard J. Crampton. 1983.

139. *T. G. Masaryk Revisited: A Cirtical Assessment.* By Hanus J. Hajek. 1983.

140. *The Cult of Power: Dictators in the Twentieth Century.* Edited by Joseph Held. 1983.

141. *Economy and Foreign Policy: The Struggle of the Great Powers for Economic Hegemony in the Danube Valley, 1919–1939.* By György Ránki. 1983.

142. *Germany, Russia, and the Balkans: Prelude to the Nazi-Soviet Non-Aggression Pact.* By Marilynn Giroux Hitchens. 1983.

143. *Guestworkers in the German Reich: The Poles in Wilhelmian Germany.* By Richard Charles Murphy. 1983.

144. *The Latvian Impact on the Bolshevik Revolution.* By Andrew Ezergailis. 1983.

145. *The Rise of Moscow's Power.* By Henryk Paszkiewicz. 1983.

146. *A Question of Empire: Leopold I and the War of the Spanish Succession, 1701–1705.* By Linda and Marsha Frey. 1983.

147. *Effects of World War I. The Uprooted: Hungarian Refugees and Their Impact on Hungarian Domestic Policies, 1918–1921.* By Istvan I. Mocsy. 1983.

148. *Nationalist Integration Through Socialist Planning: An Anthropological Study of a Romanian New Town.* By Steven L. Sampson. 1983.

149. *Decadence of Freedom: Jacques Riviere's Quest of Russian Mentality.* By Jean-Pierre Cap. 1983.

150. *East Central European Society in the Age of Revolutions, 1775-1856.* Edited by Béla K. Király. 1984.

151. *The Crucial Decade: East Central European Society and National Defense, 1859-1870.* Edited by Béla K. Király. 1984.

152. *The First War between Socialist States: The Hungarian Revolution of 1956 and Its Impact.* Edited by Béla K. Király, Barbara Lotze and Nandor Dreisziger. 1984.

153. *Russian Bolshevism and British Labor, 1917-1921.* By Morton H. Cowden. 1984.

154. *Feliks Dzierzynski and the SDKPIL: A Study of the Origins of Polish Communism.* By Robert Blobaum. 1984.

155. *Studies on Kosova.* Edited by Arshi Pipa and Sami Repishti. 1984.

156. *New Horizons in East-West Economic and Business Relations.* Edited by Marvin A. Jackson and James D. Woodson. 1984.

157. *Czech Nationalism in the Nineteenth Century.* By John F. N. Bradley. 1984.

158. *The Theory of the General Strike from the French Revolution to Poland.* By Phil H. Goodstein. 1984.

159. *King Zog and the Struggle for Stability in Albania.* By Bernd J. Fischer. 1984.

160. *Tradition and Avant-Garde: The Arts in Serbian Culture between the Two World Wars.* By Jelena Milojković-Djurić. 1984.

161. *The Megali Idea and the Greek Turkish War of 1897.* By Theodore G. Tatsios. 1984.

162. *The Hungarian Jewish Catastrophe: A Selected and Annotated Bibliography.* By Randolph L. Braham. 1984.

163. *Goli Otok—Island of Death [A Diary in Letters].* By Venko Markovski. 1984.

164. *Initiation and Initiative: An Exploration of the Life and Ideas of Dimitrije Mitrinovic.* By Andrew Rigby. 1984.

165. *Nations, Nationalities, Peoples: A Study of the Nationality Policies of the Communist Party in Soviet Moldavia.* By Michael Bruchis. 1984.

166. *Frederick I, The Man and His Times.* By Linda and Marsha Frey. 1984.

167. *The Effects of World War I: War Communism in Hungary.* By György